WORLD OF

MUMMIES
AND TOMBS

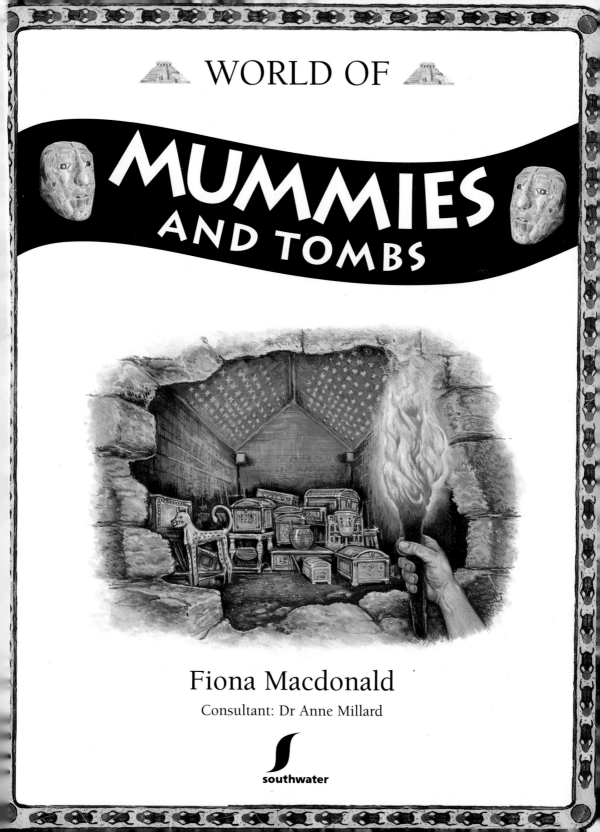

Fiona Macdonald

Consultant: Dr Anne Millard

southwater

This edition is published by Southwater

Southwater is an imprint of
Anness Publishing Limited
Hermes House
88-89 Blackfriars Road
London
SE1 8HA
tel. 020 7401 2077

Distributed in the UK by
The Manning Partnership
251-253 London Road East
Batheaston
Bath BA1 7RL
tel. 01225 852 727
fax 01225 852 852

Distributed in the USA by
Anness Publishing Inc.
27 West 20th Street
Suite 504
New York
NY 10011
tel. 212 807 6739
fax 212 807 6813

Distributed in Australia by
Sandstone Publishing
Unit 1
360 Norton Street
Leichhardt
New South Wales 2040
tel. 02 9560 7888
fax 020 7488

©2000 Anness Publishing Limited
10 9 8 7 6 5 4 3 2 1

Publisher: Joanna Lorenz
Managing Editor, Children's Books: Gilly Cameron
Cooper
Editors: Joanne Hanks, Peter Harrison
Projects Editor: Jenni Rainford
Designer: Margaret Sadler
Illustration: Peter Bull; Donato Spedaliere
Picture Research: Diana Phillips
Stylist: Melanie Williams

Anness Publishing would like to thank the following
children, and their parents, for modelling for this
book: Mark Bygraves, Alex Camfields, Colvin Ellis,
Edward Emmett, Musteyde Firket, Stephanie Follen,
John Jlitakryan, Sian Munday, Pelumi Olaosun,
Tabitha Anne Riley, Adam Christopher Williams and
Sava Yilmaz.

CONTENTS

Life After Death

Throughout human history, in civilizations across the world, people have believed that there is another world beyond this one. They have often gone to great lengths to make sure that a person's spirit lives on after death. To help this to happen, prayers have been said and elaborate ceremonies planned when someone has died. Sometimes the dead person's body is treated in special ways. For example, the Vikings cremated bodies to let spirits escape to the next world. The Tibetans placed bodies in the open air, where bitter winds and birds of prey stripped the flesh from the bones. That way, their spirit could be reborn.

In ancient Egypt, bodies were preserved so that a person's *ka* (spirit) had somewhere to live. The *ka* would not survive the afterlife if its home in the preserved body, or mummy, was allowed to decay. Other societies did not think it was so important to preserve the body as long as the spirit lived on.

To house both bodies and spirits, people who had enough money had special tombs built. When they died, food, clothes, tools, weapons and jewellery were buried alongside their corpses, to use in their new life in the next world.

▲ LAST RITES

Nearly 70 days have passed since this dead pharaoh's body arrived in the mummy-maker's workshop. Now a priest places holy amulets between the layers of linen bandages to protect the mummy from evil spirits. For this solemn task he wears the jackal-head mask of Anubis, the ancient Egyptian god of the dead.

▲ TUTANKHAMUN'S TREASURE

A splendid golden shrine surrounded the coffin of Egyptian pharaoh Tutankhamun. His tomb was found in 1922, by English archaeologist Howard Carter, after years of searching. It was filled with gilded furniture, jewellery, royal clothing and ornaments – items that the pharaoh would need in the afterlife. The royal tomb, unlike most others in Egypt, had not been disturbed or robbed since Tutankhamun's funeral, over 3,000 years earlier. Little was known about the pharaoh until the tomb's discovery.

▲ EVERYDAY AFTERLIFE

This wall painting from an Egyptian tomb, made around 1400BC, shows a group of farmworkers busy harvesting wheat and carrying sheaves to the stackyard. The Egyptians believed that life after death would be similar to life in the world of the living. So they decorated their tombs with pictures of themselves enjoying everyday activities, including working, eating and relaxing with their families and friends.

◀ DEAD BUT NOT BURIED

The mummified body of Jeremy Bentham still sits in a glass case at University College, London, more than 150 years after he died. Bentham, who lived in England from 1748–1832, was a philosopher who tried to invent ways of improving society. Before he died he gave instructions for his body to be treated in an unusual way. First, he asked his scientific friends to dissect it to increase their understanding of how the human body works. Then he wanted it to be put together again, dressed in a suit of his own clothes, topped with a wax head, and displayed in a glass case. He hoped that not only his body, but his reputation, too, would be preserved.

▲ ANCESTOR MOUND

This steep, pyramid-shaped tomb houses the body of Pacal, ruler of the Maya people of Mexico from AD615 to 683. Maya kings were buried beneath huge mud-brick mounds. Each new ruler built a mound on top of those of his ancestors, to share in their importance. Over the centuries, the tomb-mounds became taller as more kings were buried. Each one was topped by a temple, where priests made offerings to the dead to communicate with their spirits.

▲ ON GUARD FOREVER

This carriage and its horses were put with terracotta (baked clay) soldiers in an emperor's tomb to serve him in the afterlife. The first Chinese emperor, Shi Huangdi, died around 207BC. He was an extremely powerful man and expected to enjoy the same power and high position after death as he had in life. His underground tomb was discovered by accident in 1974 when local people were digging a well. They found three large pits containing a vast array of life-size terracotta equipment and over 7,000 soldiers. Every one of the soldiers in the terracotta army had an individual face.

PRESERVED BY ACCIDENT ▶

The body of British explorer John Torrington was mummified by the cold, dry winds of the Arctic. He died, probably in 1846, of frostbite and hunger with all the other members of an expedition led by Sir John Franklin. They were searching for the Northwest Passage, a seaway around the top of North America. Natural mummies have been found in many parts of the world. Some have been frozen, while others have been dried out by wind and sand, or preserved in peat bogs.

Sail into the Afterlife

A beautiful, boat-shaped funeral bark (barge) ferried the mummified body of a dead pharoah to its final resting place on the West Bank of the Nile. After use, the funeral barge was placed in the dead pharaoh's tomb, or buried close by. The ancient Egyptians believed that the boat would also carry the dead pharaoh's spirit through the Underworld. The barges used in funeral ceremonies were copies of holy, boat-shaped shrines in temples, and were sometimes carried in processions on festival days. The model boat in this project is based on a boat-shrine dedicated to Amun, the creator god.

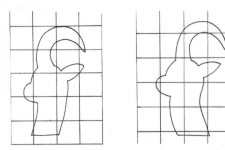

1 Use a soft pencil and a ruler to draw a grid made up of 2cm squares on the card. Then use the grid to help you copy the two designs shown above, so that you have two of each. Copy the outline a square at a time. Use scissors to cut out the traced designs to form the two templates for an antelope's head.

You will need: soft-leaded pencil, ruler, 4 pieces of A4 thin white card, scissors, newspaper, masking tape, 250g plain flour, 200ml tap water, bowl, fork, fine sandpaper, medium and fine paintbrushes, white, red, black, blue, gold and green acrylic paints, white spirit, wood varnish, kebab stick, empty camera film box, 4 pieces of dowel 1cm in diameter and about 40cm long, PVA glue.

6 Dip the strips of newspaper in the paste. Cover the boat in the strips. Only cover up to the neck of the antelope heads. Leave to dry for several hours.

7 When the model is dry, smooth the boat surface with fine sandpaper. Shake off the dust into a sink. Make sure the boat is very smooth.

8 Use the thicker paintbrush to apply a white base to coat the boat. This will give the boat a uniform background. Brush the strokes in the same direction.

Chensumose, priest of Amun, sails through the Underworld, hoping to find his way past all its dangers. This picture is from a papyrus scroll buried in Chensumose's tomb around 1000BC. His family put it beside his body, for him to use as a guidebook to the Underworld, and to remind him of spells he might need.

12 Use a fine paintbrush to paint the oars. Blend the green and blue paints to make a turquoise colour. Follow the pattern shown above.

13 Paint an empty camera box film white. Glue 4 pieces of dowel to the corners of the empty camera film box to make a sarcophagus (coffin).

2 Tear newspaper into strips. Scrunch them roughly into the shape of a boat's hull. Squeeze the ends together to make them narrower.

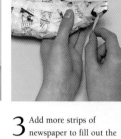

3 Add more strips of newspaper to fill out the hull shape. Wind masking tape all over the hull and mould the ends into a point.

4 Stick two antelope's heads to each end of the boat with masking tape. Place the pairs of heads so that they face in the same direction.

5 Mix the flour and water in a bowl with a fork to make a thick but runny paste. Tear some more of the newspaper into strips.

9 Decorate the boat using the red, black, blue, gold and green acrylic paints. Use the thinner paintbrush and black paint to outline and detail areas.

10 Leave the painted boat to dry for at least an hour. Clean the thicker paintbrush in white spirit and use it to varnish the boat with the wood varnish.

11 Cut out two double petal shapes from the leftover white card. Bend each petal and push a kebab stick through the centre, as shown.

The green of the boat represents the colour of crops before they ripen. To the Egyptians, this was a sign of rebirth and new life after death. They hoped the funeral barge would carry them safely from this world to the next.

14 Decorate the sarcophagus with gold, blue, red, green and black paint. Stick two pieces of card together to make a canopy (roof) and paint it too.

15 Stick the canopy on the sarcophagus. Place the sarcophagus on the boat. Glue the oars to the back of the boat to make the finished barge.

A Global Custom

The best-known mummies were made in ancient Egypt between about 3000BC and AD200. However, people from many other civilizations also honoured their dead by mummifying them. To help dead leaders, relatives and friends find everlasting life, they preserved their bodies and built monumental tombs where they could rest undisturbed for ever. Archaeologists have found mummified bodies in sites as far apart as Greenland, Italy, Siberia, China and Peru. Splendid tombs full of buried treasures have also been uncovered all around the world, from northern Europe to West Africa, South America and the Middle East.

Each civilization developed its own funeral ceremonies and burial customs as part of its religion. People used different techniques to preserve bodies and to build tombs, depending on available materials and the skills of local craftworkers. Whatever civilization they came from, mummies and tombs were made for the same two reasons. They were made either by people who wanted to make sure that no-one forgot them after death, or by those who wanted to remember their own dead.

Greenland

NORTH AMERICA

SOUTH AMERICA

◀ **FAMILY TOMB**
A massive, dome-shaped tomb called a *tholos* was designed to house the bodies of a whole family. It also served as a proud monument. This is one of many hundreds built by the Myceneans, a warrior people who lived in southern Greece from around 1600BC. Within each tomb, older corpses were moved aside from time to time, to make room for fresh burials. Personal items, such as weapons, jewellery, or even children's toys, were buried alongside each body.

KEY
1. Natural mummy, Canada
2. Inuit mummy, Greenland
3. Pyramid of the Sun, Mexico
4. Mummy from Sipan, Peru
5. Tomb of Pacal, Mexico
6. Bog man, Denmark
7. Royal tombs of Mycenae, Greece
8. Pyramids at Giza, Egypt
9. Mummy in frozen earth, Siberia
10. Tomb of Shi Huangdi, China
11. Dried mummy, Indonesia

RUSSIAN FEDERATION

6

EUROPE

9 CHINA

7

10

8

INDIA

AFRICA

Indonesia

11

N

AUSTRALIA

Through the Ages

For thousands of years human beings have treated their dead with respect. The earliest-known human graves – in a cave at Qafzeh, Israel – date from around 100,000BC. Later prehistoric people made beds of grass and flowers for dead bodies to rest on. They scattered the bodies with red ochre (earth) and arranged personal belongings beside them.

The first mummies were made much later. The oldest-surviving ones were made by the Chinchorro people of South America from around 3500BC. Like the ancient Egyptians, the Chinchorro people noticed that dead bodies buried in sand were preserved. The mummy-makers aimed to learn from nature and create more lifelike images of the dead. In ancient Egypt from 3000BC mummy-makers tried to improve their techniques, trying out different ways of drying flesh, and adding bodypaint, masks and elaborate wrappings.

From AD300 to 900, the Maya of Central America tried to preserve bodies of important people by covering them with jade or gold and burying them in strong, stone tombs.

▲ WORLD'S OLDEST MUMMY?
This mummy has survived for almost 5,000 years. It was made by the ancient Chinchorro people, from the Atacama Desert region of present-day Chile and Peru. Chinchorro mummies are the oldest ever discovered. They were made by being skinned, taken apart and heat-dried, then tied back together. The body was supported with sticks and padding, such as clay or feathers. It was coated in white paste made from ashes, and the dried facial skin and hair was put on, like a mask.

▲ A GOLDEN CASE
The gilded coffin of a priestess of the sun god Amun is from the period about 1550 to 945BC. This was a time when Egyptian mummy-makers had reached the peak of their skills. On the front of the coffin, an idealized portrait of the priestess shows her as a young and attractive woman. The coffins of rich people had several layers. Each one was covered with pictures of gods and inscriptions of magic spells to protect the dead person.

◄ ANCIENT GREEK SPLENDOUR
A circle of graves at Mycenae that contains six royal burials. Some of the most lavish tomb treasures in the world were buried with the warrior kings of Mycenae. This wealthy trading city in southern Greece was powerful from around 1600BC. Members of the ruling family were buried in clothes, with a vast quantity of gold in the form of jewellery, drinking vessels, burial masks and decorated weapons. One of the royal skeletons excavated at Mycenae was surrounded by 5kg of gold.

▲ THE SUTTON HOO TREASURE

A warrior's helmet was one of the treasures found at the Sutton Hoo ship burial in England. In the AD600s, Anglo-Saxon kings and lords were often buried in their ships, which were dragged on to land. They were surrounded by treasures to take with them to the afterlife. The beautiful ornaments that filled the Sutton Hoo ship were made both in England and abroad. The helmet probably came from Sweden.

CITY OF THE DEAD ▶

Mummy-bundles sit surrounded by skulls at the bottom of a stone-lined underground chamber at Cahuachi, in southern Peru. The Nazca people flourished there during the first and second centuries AD. During the AD100s they built huge earth-mounds and pyramids at Cahuachi. But they never actually lived in the city. It was a religious and ceremonial centre, used only for burying their dead.

.▲ INSIDE A ROYAL TOMB

Archaeologists excavating at Vergina in Macedonia found this large tomb packed with gold, silver and ivory treasures. Inside a marble sarcophagus (stone coffin) was a gold chest containing the cremated remains of a man. They were covered in a purple cloak and a gold oak wreath. Tiny bits of the skull matched portraits of King Philip II of Macedon, father of Alexander the Great, who conquered an empire around 330BC.

▲ DRESSED FOR DEATH

These Sicilian mummies are still dressed in the clothes in which they were buried more than 200 years ago. The Sicilian people of southern Italy had a tradition of burying their dead in underground rock corridors, called catacombs. In the cold dry air of the catacombs, the mummies of their ancestors have survived to this day.

Preserving the Dead

A dead body will rot if it is left out in the open, enclosed in a coffin, or buried in damp earth. The skin, muscles and internal organs decay, leaving only the bony skeleton and the teeth. In certain types of soil, even these disappear, leaving only an imprint on the ground, or nothing at all. Where bodies do survive, it is because they have been buried in extremely dry, wet or cold conditions which help to preserve them.

Mummy-makers invented many techniques to prevent the process of decay, such as drying, smoking, freezing or embalming corpses by injecting them with special substances. The ancient Egyptians washed the corpse and removed the internal organs. They removed the brain, but left the heart (which was where, they believed, thinking went on) inside. The body and organs were packed with crystals of natron, a salty chemical, and left to dry for about 35 days. For another 35 days the body was padded with wads of linen and tightly wrapped in layers of resin-soaked bandages. Only after the 70 days was the finished mummy placed in a coffin.

▲ SLEEPING IN SAND

An Egyptian man lies curled up in a peaceful sleeping position, just as his family arranged his dead body about 5,000 years ago. Early Egyptian burials were simple – just a shallow grave to contain the body. A few treasured possessions were arranged around the body and sand was heaped on top. The dryness of the desert climate stopped the body from rotting away. Throughout the ancient Egyptian period, most ordinary people continued to be buried in this way. Rich people who were mummified paid for it to be done.

BURIED IN A PEAT BOG ▶

A peat bog preserved the body of this Iron Age man from Denmark. The natural acidity of the bog water and the lack of air prevented decay by stopping bacteria growing. He was thrown into the bog around 200BC, after being strangled, possibly as a human sacrifice. His skin, hair, flesh and internal organs survive, but his bones are reduced to a spongy mass.

◀ WIND-DRIED MUMMY

A Peruvian mummy is wrapped in a woven cloth and headdress ready for life after death. The Paracas people of Peru lived from about 600 to 100BC. They buried their dead in two types of burial chambers. Some were the deserted underground homes of a people who had lived in the same region before them. Others were bottle-shaped chambers dug several metres underground. The dried-out bodies were placed on open, saucer-like baskets, and wrapped in layers of colourful cloth.

◀ VOLCANIC VICTIM

A plaster cast preserves the outline of a man who died at Pompeii, Italy in AD79. The city was buried under volcanic ash as nearby Mount Vesuvius erupted. Many people were killed by clouds of burning ash and poison gas. Over the centuries, the ash solidified and the bodies rotted away, leaving hollow spaces where they had been.

TOOLS OF THE MUMMY-MAKERS ▶

A figure of Anubis, the dog-headed god who watched over ancient Egyptian undertakers, decorates this bronze embalming knife. Sharp knives were used to open up dead bodies. A cut about 10cm long was made near the left hip to remove the lungs, liver, intestines and stomach. Removing the internal organs helped to stop the rest of the flesh rotting away. Many different tools were used by the highly-skilled mummy-makers. For example, the brain was removed by forcing a hook through the nose and then scraping out the inside of the skull.

BEST FACE FORWARD ▶

Mummies made after Egypt became a province of the Roman Empire in 30BC were decorated with portraits of the dead person. Unlike the idealized masks painted on ancient Egyptian mummies, the Roman-Egyptian faces are extremely realistic. This boy's portrait was probably painted while he was still alive. Roman-Egyptian mummies were less skilfully made than earlier Egyptian ones. The internal organs were left inside and the body was pumped full of resin. It was a quicker and cheaper method.

◀ KEEPING UP APPEARANCES

The unwrapped head of an Egyptian mummy shows the skin, teeth and hair perfectly preserved. The process of embalming made the flesh look withered and discoloured. To keep the features as natural as possible, small wads of linen were inserted under the skin to give a plump, lifelike look. The natron (salt) used to preserve the body also destroyed the eyes, so the eye sockets were stuffed with pads and the lids closed over them.

Extra Storage

Egyptian mummy-makers removed the body's internal organs and stored them in special containers called canopic jars. There were four canopic jars, one each for the lungs, intestines, liver and stomach. A jackal-headed jar like the one in this project would have held the stomach. The organs could not be thrown away because they were part of the body and might have been used by a magician in a spell against the dead person. Mummy-makers in other countries also removed organs from dead bodies, filling the empty space with sweet-smelling herbs and spices, clay, sand, salt, cloth or straw.

1 Use a ruler and pencil to draw a rectangle measuring 6 x 26cm on the white card. Go round the outline of the rectangle in black marker pen.

2 Use scissors to cut out the shape you have drawn. This is the beginning of the lid. Cut as straight as possible, as this will help the lid fit on the jar.

5 The dome is finished when all the slits have been bent inwards. Secure the dome using masking tape. The dome will form the lid of your canopic jar.

6 Tear newspaper into strips and scrunch into a ball about 4cm diameter (about the size of a golf ball). Cover in masking tape to form the head.

7 Cut triangular ears about 4 x 2.5cm from card. Roll a strip of newspaper into a tube to make the muzzle. Use masking tape to stick these to the head.

8 Hold the base of the lid firmly in one hand. With the other, tape strips of masking tape over the head and dome. The Jackal's head is ready for pasting.

You will need: ruler, pencil, thin white card, black marker pen, scissors, masking tape, newspaper, bowl, plain flour, water, fork, three paper cups (about 10cm tall and 7.5cm in diameter), fine sandpaper, cloth, white emulsion paint, paintbrushes, cream, green, blue, gold, white and black acrylic paints, clear wood varnish.

11 When both the jar and lid are completely dry, sand the outsides down with fine sandpaper until smooth. Dust them with a cloth.

12 Paint the inside and out of the jar and lid with white emulsion. Paint the outside of the jar with cream acrylic paint, leaving a rim of white at the top.

13 Mix green, blue and white paints to make turquoise. Use this to paint the head. Paint blue and gold stripes on the dome. Draw a face on the head.

3 Mark 1cm spaces along one side of the card. Cut 4cm in to the card at each of the 1cm marks you have drawn. This will make a row of slits.

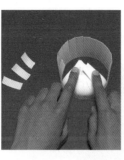

4 Bend each of the slits inwards to make a dome shape. Then stick each strip down with small fingertip-sized squares of masking tape.

9 Put 250g of plain flour into a bowl. Pour in enough water to make a batter-like paste, mixing with a fork. Tear more newspaper into strips.

10 Dip the strips in the paste. Cover the lid with three layers of paper. Stack three paper cups together and cover them with paste, inside and out.

14 Draw a spell on the body of the jar using a pencil. Copy the design shown above or look for references for other spells in books on Egypt.

15 Paint the face in black and white and the spell on the jar in black. Paint the top rim gold and leave it to dry for 2 hours, then varnish it.

This human-headed silver canopic jar is one of a set made for the pharaoh Shoshenq II around 890BC. The jackal, baboon, hawk and human heads were representations of four minor Egyptian gods, called the Sons of Horus. In later times, the mummy-makers began to pack the dried, wrapped internal organs back inside a mummy's body, before bandaging it. They continued to put dummy canopic jars in each tomb because of the god's protective power. The mummy-makers wanted to be as sure as possible that the mummified person would survive in the next world.

Jackal-headed jars were used to hold a dead person's stomach. Human-headed jars were for the liver, baboon-headed jars for lungs and hawk-headed jars were for intestines. Real jars were usually made from stone, wood or pottery.

Who was Mummified?

People believed that being made into a mummy greatly increased the chances of living for ever. Yet, in most civilizations, this opportunity was open only to the lucky few. Whether your body was mummified or not often depended on how rich and powerful you were, or how useful you might be to an important dead person in the next world. Rich people, such as Egyptian pharaohs, nobles, priests and their wives, paid a great deal of money to expert mummy-makers. They hired priests to perform elaborate funeral ceremonies in the correct way. Pharaohs often gave orders for work to begin on their own temples and tombs long before they died, and spent fortunes collecting treasures to be buried alongside their bodies.

In other civilizations, such as ancient China and Sumer (in present-day Iraq), the wives, servants and bodyguards of powerful people were often killed and buried alongside their masters and mistresses, so that they would be able to serve and entertain them in the next world. Beautiful people, such as young Inca girls of Peru, were sometimes killed and mummified as sacrifices to the gods.

▲ LORD OF SIPAN
The lid of the wooden coffin in which rests the Lord of Sipán is lowered slowly into the deep grave. He will lie here in the dry earth of Northern Peru for centuries until grave-robbers discover his tomb and steal his gold. Not even kings keep riches forever.

◄ SERVING THE GODS
The red straps around this mummy case, which was buried around 1085BC, show that it was designed for a priestess. She is prepared for the passage into the afterlife. Her hands hold offerings for the gods of the underworld. All over the inside and outside of the case, there are spells and ritual verses to safeguard the priestess's journey to the underworld. Priests and priestesses devoted their lives to serving the gods in their temples. Often they came from noble families. Important priests and priestesses usually had their own special tombs.

▼ CHILD OF THE ICE
A young child was accidentally mummified in the Arctic ice of Greenland about 600 years ago. The Inuit people of Greenland laid their dead to rest in quiet caves. The bodies were dressed in warm clothing for their journey to the land of the dead. Bodies buried in summer slowly rotted away, but those buried during the bitter winters soon froze solid. The caves acted like a refrigerator, keeping the bodies cold enough not to thaw again, even in summer.

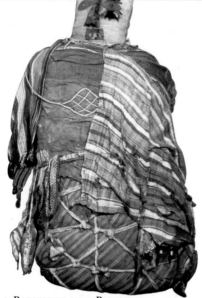

FROZEN FOR THE FUTURE ▶

This strange-looking piece of scientific equipment is part of a cryogenic storage system. It is designed to keep bodies chilled and preserved. Today, a few very rich people have paid large sums of money to have their bodies stored this way, in tanks of super-cooled liquid gas. They hope they may be restored to life many years from now, when scientists have discovered how to thaw their bodies and make their vital organs work again. No-one knows whether it will ever be done.

▲ PRESERVED IN A PALACE

The Chimu people, who lived in the northern Andes mountains from around AD1000, turned the bodies of their kings into mummy-bundles. They dressed the body in gold ornaments and wrapped it in fine cloth. Kings were buried at the Chimu capital of Chanchan, Peru. Each king was buried in the centre of his own palace compound, which became his tomb. The next king to rule built a new palace, to be his home both in life and death.

ENEMY TROPHY ▼

The heads of enemies killed in battle were preserved by headhunters in Ecuador. Trophy heads, such as this one from about 100 years ago, were valued as a source of magic power. The heads were preserved by smoking or heat-drying. Eyes and mouth were pinned tight shut, the brain was removed and holes were drilled through the skull so that a carrying rope could be threaded through.

◀ TUTANKHAMUN'S MASK

This mask of solid gold and lapis lazuli (a semi-precious stone) shows that the mummy beneath is that of a rich and powerful person. It is a portrait of the Egyptian pharaoh Tutankhamun, depicted as the sun god, Re. The pharaoh wears a cobra and vulture headdress and a false beard, both signs of his kingship.

Symbols of Royalty

Rich and powerful people were almost always buried with evidence of their status (position). The mummies of pharaohs were sent to the afterlife with signs of royal authority. A crook symbolized kingship, a flail represented Egypt's fertile land and a false beard was a sign of their god-like power. The three projects shown here will show you how to make these three symbols of royal power. From around 2000BC, the mummies and tombs of Egyptian pharaohs were also identified by a cartouche – an oval outline with the pharaoh's royal name and title inscribed in the centre.

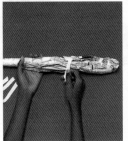

1 Take the 53cm length of dowel. Wind sheets of scrunched up newspaper over it overlapping the end by 35cm. Secure it using masking tape.

2 Wrap more tape around the newspaper to make a neat and strong crook. To bend it, stick a piece of tape across the inside curve to hold the bend in place.

You will need: Crook: 53cm length of dowel, newspaper, masking tape, 200g plain flour, 200ml water, glass bowl, fine sandpaper, paintbrush, blue paint, gold paint. Beard: newspaper, masking tape, 1 x 40cm black ribbon, scissors, 10 x 30cm black felt, 2.5 x 45cm black felt, PVA glue and brush. Flail: 48cm length of dowel (2.5cm diameter), masking tape, newspaper, 200g plain flour, 200ml water, glass bowl, fine sandpaper, paintbrush, blue paint, gold paint, 3 pieces of 26cm dowel, white thread, self-hardening clay, cocktail stick, needle.

BEARD

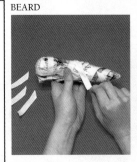

1 Scrunch up newspaper to form a large, fat carrot-like shape. Use masking tape to secure your basic design together and to shape it.

2 Tape the centre of the black ribbon to the top of the shape. Cut the large black felt in to four 2 x 6cm pieces. Fold these over the top of the shape and tape in place.

3 Tape the other two pieces of felt over the bottom of the shape. This will neaten the ends and ensure your beard shape is competely covered.

FLAIL

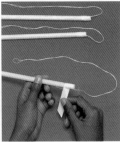

1 Take the 48cm length of dowel 2.5cm in diameter. Tape scrunched up newspaper to overlap one end by 30cm. Bend the newspaper into a hook shape.

2 Mix up a paste of flour and water. Tear newspaper into strips. Dip the strips in the paste and cover the hook shape with three layers of papier mâché.

3 When it is dry, smooth the shape down with a piece of fine sandpaper. Use a fine paintbrush to paint the flail with a band of blue and gold.

4 Take three pieces of dowel, 1cm in diameter, 26cm long. Tape a double thickness of white thread about 30cm long to the end of each dowel.

3 Mix a paste of flour and water. Tear up strips of newspaper and dip them in the paste. Wrap three layers to make papier mâché around the hook.

4 Leave to dry. Smooth the surface with fine sandpaper. Paint bands of blue and gold as shown in Step 3 of the Flail project below.

The god Osiris, king of the Underworld, is shown here sitting on a throne, as if he were a living pharaoh. Like all Egyptian kings, he carries a crook and a flail as signs of his royal authority. Pictures such as this were painted inside coffins and tombs as a way of honouring Osiris's power and asking for his blessing.

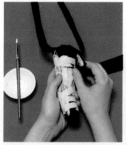

4 Cut a length of black felt about 2.5 x 45cm. Dab PVA glue on one end and attach to the top of the shape. Wrap it down the shape, overlapping as you go.

5 When you reach the bottom of the beard shape, cut off any felt left over. Add a little dab of glue to the end and neatly glue the end down to cover any gaps.

Crooks and flails were decorated with gold and precious stones like many other royal treasures.

5 Shape self-hardening clay into 15 little cone-like beads. Make a hole through the centre of each one with a cocktail stick. Leave the clay to dry completely.

6 Use a fine paintbrush to paint nine of the cone-shaped beads blue and the other six gold. Paint the three dowelling rods with gold paint.

7 Thread the cotton from each dowel through a needle. Thread five alternate beads on each. Sew these to the end of the flail and knot them several times.

Gods of the Dead

The ancient Egyptians worshipped many gods and goddesses. Re, the sun god, was the source of life on Earth. Horus was the god of the sky and Hathor the mother god, while Osiris was king of the Underworld. Jackal-headed Anubis was protector of tombs and cemeteries. He also watched over mummy-makers and guided dead spirits through the terrifying ordeals of the journey through the Underworld. The goddess Maat (Truth) judged dead people's hearts, and decided whether they deserved to survive. The Egyptians worshipped all these gods with prayers, music, dancing and offerings of food.

In many other civilizations, such as in North and South America, people worshipped gods who demanded sacrifices of living people and animals, in return for keeping the world alive. Some ancient peoples believed that gods controlled the world of the dead. The Romans thought that dead spirits lived in a misty, miserable land ruled by the stern god Hades. The Celtic peoples of north-west Europe feared the Morrigan, a sinister, shape-changing goddess of battles and death. They also believed that, in the spirit world, a dead warrior cooked in a magic cauldron overnight would be restored to life.

▲ **JACKAL-HEADED GOD**
Anubis, the Egyptian god who protected the dead, was usually shown with a jackal or dog's head. Jackals were often found in cemeteries, where they would dig up dead bodies unless they were driven away. Statues of Anubis were usually painted black, which was the colour of the Nile's sticky mud. For the Egyptians this was the colour of fertility and new life after death.

◄ **UNDERWORLD**
A statue of gold and lapis lazuli shows Osiris, the king of the Egyptian Underworld, flanked by his wife Isis and Horus, their hawk-headed son. Osiris also ruled over a peaceful land called the Field of the Reeds. Here, dead spirits who had safely completed their dangerous journey from the world of the living, could enjoy eternal life.

▲ **OFFERINGS TO A MIGHTY GOD**
A Celtic god gazes out from a silver cauldron, found at Gundestrup in Denmark. On either side of him are figures of a man and a woman, who have been killed as sacrifices. The cauldron was broken into many pieces then thrown into a bog as an offering to the gods nearly 2,000 years ago. The Celts made many offerings of humans, animals and treasures to ask their gods for help.

◀ FERTILE MOTHER-GODDESS

Aztec people believed that if they fed the gods with human blood, the gods would protect them. This statue of the fertility goddess Coatlicue is decorated with the skulls of sacrificed victims. According to legend, the goddess was attacked by her jealous daughter while she was pregnant with Huitzilopochtli, the Aztec tribal god. He jumped out of her body as a fully-formed warrior and killed his sister, who then became the first human sacrifice. The Aztec gods represented the forces of nature. They could nourish humans by sending rain, or kill them by withholding it.

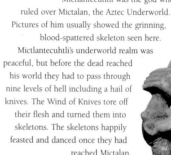

A WELCOME SMILE ▶

Mictlantecuhtli was the god who ruled over Mictalan, the Aztec Underworld. Pictures of him usually showed the grinning, blood-spattered skeleton seen here. Mictlantecuhtli's underworld realm was peaceful, but before the dead reached his world they had to pass through nine levels of hell including a hail of knives. The Wind of Knives tore off their flesh and turned them into skeletons. The skeletons happily feasted and danced once they had reached Mictalan.

◀ THE WAY OF THE DEAD

At the heart of the ancient Mexican city of Teotihuacan is the temple-lined avenue known as the Way of the Dead. People honoured the spirits of their dead ancestors at tombs along this 8km-long main street. For more than 1,000 years Teotihuacan was Mexico's holiest city. In AD600 it was the sixth largest city in the world. Around AD650 Teotihuacan was attacked and burned. Its citizens mostly fled but the temples survived, along with the memory of the ancestor spirits who had lived in the tombs. For this reason, later peoples, such as the Aztecs, who visited Teotihuacan as a place of pilgrimage, gave the Way of the Dead its name.

Mask of a God

Hawk-headed Horus was the Egyptian god of the sky. His bright, all-seeing eyes, like those of a bird of prey, represented the sun and the moon. His name means "He who is far above". Horus was also the special protector of Egyptian rulers. Pharaohs were often portrayed with a hawk or falcon hovering above them. There are many myths about Horus and his fights with other gods. One tells of a fight with Seth, his uncle, when he lost his left eye. He was healed by Thoth, the god of medicine, who managed to return the missing eye to him. This project shows you how to make a mask based on Horus's head.

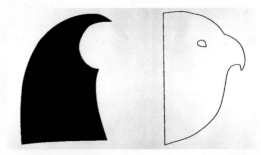

1 The two outlines shown above are the face and hood of the mask. Copy the shapes using a pencil and ruler to draw each of the outlines on to two pieces of A3 thick white card. Carefully mark over these outlines with a black felt-tipped pen. Using a pair of scissors, carefully cut out each of the shapes you have drawn.

You will need: *pencil, two pieces of A3 thick white card, black felt tipped pen, scissors, two pieces of A3 thin white card, paintbrushes, PVA glue, masking tape, yellow, black, red and gold acrylic paints, ruler, 1m square black fabric, dress-making pins, sewing needle, cotton thread, red fabric.*

6 Bend up the tabs on each shape and brush the edges of them with glue. Do this on both halves, make sure you glue the inner sides so they fit together.

7 Stick the two shapes together, on one side. The tabs stick to the other half of the mask. Tape the edges by the tabs to secure the mask until the glue is dry.

8 Using a medium-size paintbrush and the bright yellow acrylic paint, colour both sides of the mask shape bright yellow.

These carvings of Horus march along the walls of the temple of Ramesses II at Abydos. Ramesses ruled Egypt from 1290 to 1224BC. Many Egyptian gods were portrayed with the heads of birds or animals. The animals' special qualities represented the gods' special powers. For example, the hawk's keen eyesight represented Horus's all-seeing eyes. Hawks and other birds of prey were mummified, and left as offerings to Horus.

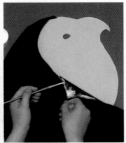

13 Turn the sewn fabric inside out. Glue the front edge of the hood. Fit on to the yellow mask, matching the head shapes on both sides. Leave to dry.

14 Draw in face detail with a pencil using the final mask as a guide. Use a fine paintbrush and black and red paints to colour in the detail.

2 Place the outline of the head shape on the A3 thin white card. Use a pencil to draw around the shape. This gives you a second template.

3 Draw the tabs in pencil around the edge of the shape. Mark these at 5cm points and make them 1cm square. Cut out the shape and around the tabs.

4 Draw around the tabbed shape to fit exactly on top of the one you have drawn. Mark tabs in between the ones in the first shape.

5 Carefully cut out the second new shape. Make sure you cut around the tabs. Each of your two shapes should have tabs in different positions.

9 Make a mark 11cm in from the beak and 7cm down from the top of the head on each side. Cut two holes to see out of at these marks, each 2.5cm across.

10 Put the hood template on to a doubled-up piece of 1m square of black fabric. Pin on the template carefully with dress-making pins.

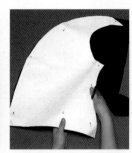

11 Use scissors to carefully cut round the outside of the hood template on the black fabric as shown. This will create two pieces of material.

12 Thread a needle with 100cm of cotton. Use a running stitch to sew only the back edge of the two pieces of fabric together.

15 Cut a piece of red fabric 5 x 44cm and glue along the bottom edge of the hood. Cut a small slit on each side of the hood and paint three gold stripes.

As you look through the eye-holes in your Horus mask, remember that hawks are famous for their keen eyesight. Egyptians carried little amulets (lucky charms) in the shape of Horus's eye. The word for them was udjat, which means healing or protection. They symbolized Horus's eye, torn out by Seth in the struggle for the throne of Egypt. Archaeologists have found thousands of udjat amulets wrapped in Egyptian mummy bandages to keep danger away.

An Animal's Afterlife

A rchaeologists have found the remains of many different
animals made into mummies or simply buried in tombs.
Some were put there because they were believed to be sacred,
and living representatives of gods. When they died, they were
buried with special ceremonies. But most animals that have
been found in tombs and graves were put there to be useful. In
death, as in life, they were meant to serve as companions and
helpers to their owners.

Sometimes, live animals were sacrificed because people
thought this was what the gods demanded. In return, they
believed the gods would give help and protection. In ancient
Greece and Rome, sacrificed animals were cremated. In Central
America, their bodies were thrown into deep wells or pits.

For thousands of years, human beings have depended on
animals for food, clothing, and for pulling carts and ploughs.
As a result, the bodies of dead animals have often been treated
with respect. The Celtic chieftains of northern Europe valued
horses so much that they gave them almost-human burials.

▲ **SPIRIT PATH**

A camel stands watchfully beside a spirit path – a walkway
leading to holy ground surrounding a Chinese tomb. This path
at Shisanling, north of Beijing, is lined with statues of animals.
Guardian statues of people, animals or imaginary monsters were
arranged along spirit paths to protect the emperors in the
afterlife. The camel was chosen as a subject for a statue
because it was valued for its strength.

◄ **SITTING PRETTY**

Stripped of its bandages the body of a
mummified baboon remains fixed in a
lifelike sitting position. It was arranged
like this thousands of years ago by Egyptian
mummy-makers. Baboons were sacred to Thoth,
god of the moon. They were kept as temple
pets and mummified when they died. Their
bodies were buried in wooden
shrines set into
wall niches in the
underground gallery
of the holy ani-
mal cemetery
at Saqqara.

▲ **A GOD ON EARTH**

A specially-chosen bull, called the Apis Bull, carries a pharaoh's
mummy through the Underworld. To the Egyptians, the Apis
Bull was sacred to the god Ptah, patron of craftsmen. It was
believed to possess the power to foretell the future and also
protect the dead. When an Apis Bull died, its funeral was a very
solemn occasion. The mummified body was buried in a granite
sarcophagus (coffin) in an underground vault called the
Serapeum, alongside all the earlier Apis Bulls.

AN OFFERING FOR THOTH ▶

These mummified heads of ibises
(tall wading birds) were found
buried in jars in the animal cemetery
at Saqqara in Egypt. Because their curved
beaks looked like the crescent-shaped new moon, ibises
were honoured as symbols of the moon god, Thoth. The priests gathered
the bodies of ibises that had died naturally. To kill them was punishable by
death. Pilgrims visiting Thoth's temple brought ibis mummies to bury
as offerings. Over four million ibis mummies have been found so far.

GUARD OF HONOUR ▶

A massive elephant stands watch over the tombs of Ming Dynasty
emperors near Beijing, China. Thirteen emperors were buried there
between around AD1400 and 1600. The elephant, a symbol of
power, is one member of an honour guard of real and mythological
creatures, all carved in stone, that stand beside the Sacred Road
running in between the tombs. They were put there to warn off
any evil spirits that might try to harm the tombs' inhabitants, and
perhaps to deter tomb robbers, as well.

▲ PREHISTORIC MUMMY

Sometimes animals were mummified by accident. This is a
plaster cast taken from the body of a dead baby mammoth,
that lived about 40,000 years ago in Siberia, now part of the
Russian Federation. This was during the last Ice Age when
large parts of the Northern Hemisphere were very much colder
than they are today. The mammoth's body froze soon after it
died and was preserved for thousands of years by layers of ice
and snow. It was found in 1977 and nicknamed Diana.
Mammoths died out 10,000 years ago, but examples such as
this allow scientists to study their organs, muscles and brains.

▲ FROM SACRED POOLS

A mummified crocodile sits on a stretcher resting on a wooden support. The
Egyptians greatly feared crocodiles, because they killed many bathers, farmers and
fishermen along the banks of the Nile. To try and tame their savagery, the Egyptians
decided to honour crocodiles as symbols of the god Sobek. Priests at Sobek's
temples kept pools of sacred crocodiles, which they fed with food offerings, and
dressed in jewels. They mummified the sacred crocodiles' bodies when they died.

An Animal Offering

Mummified cats, rather like the decorative model in this project, were beautifully wrapped in linen bandages. They were buried as offerings to the Egyptian goddess Bastet. Bastet was the daughter of Re, the sun god, and symbolized the power of the sun to ripen crops. She was often portrayed as a cat-headed woman with kittens at her feet. In Bastet's temple a sacred cat was kept, which was mummified after it died. In Egyptian homes, cats were valued for their ability to catch mice. For fun, this project includes a model mouse for you to make as food for your model cat.

1 Scrunch several sheets of newspaper into a ball. Press together and secure with masking tape. Make a smaller nose shape and stick to the head with tape.

2 Draw two triangular shaped ears in pencil on white card as shown. They should be 4cm wide and 4.5cm tall. Carefully cut out the ears.

You will need: *newspaper, masking tape, pencil, scissors, thin white card, ruler, 250g plain flour, 200ml water, fork, bowl, white fabric, PVA glue, paste brush, black, brown and yellow acrylic paints, paintbrush.*

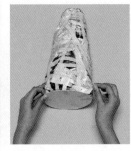

4 Roll up lots more newspaper into a tall cone shape to make the cat's body. Wrap strips of masking tape firmly around the body.

5 Place the body on card and draw around the base in pencil. Cut out the base. Stick it to the bottom of the body with masking tape.

6 Stick the head on to the body with masking tape. Make sure it is evenly placed and not wobbly by placing strips of tape all round the neck.

Cats were honoured throughout ancient Egypt. They guarded farmers' grain stores, and were loved as family pets. From around 1985BC, pictures of cats were often included in tomb paintings – in scenes of hunting and wild-fowling, or crouching under their owners' chairs.

10 Cut several much longer strips of bandage. Place the middle of one at the neck. Wrap it diagonally over the front of the body as shown and glue.

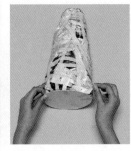

11 Turn the cat over on its back and continue the diagonal crossover wrapping of the bandages. Secure at the base with glue and masking tape.

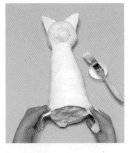

12 Wrap bandages over the remainder of the cat's body as shown. Glue the bandage ends in postion until the cat is entirely covered.

3 Lay the head on the work surface. Place each ear in line on the back of the head. Stick masking tape on either side fo each ear to join to the head.

MOUSE MODEL

1 Use self-hardening clay to make a pointed oval shape for the mouse's body. Make two petal shapes for the ears. Use fingers to smooth to the head.

2 Roll out a small piece of clay for a tail and four balls for feet. Use a modelling tool to make eyes and a fur pattern on the mouse's back.

3 Make a box shape from a rectangle of the clay. Draw a line around the top of the box to look like a lid. Place the mouse on top of the box.

4 Leave the clay to harden overnight. When completely dry, paint in metallic colours to make the mouse and coffin look like bronze metal.

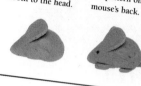

7 Mix a paste of flour and water. Tear newspaper into strips and smear them with paste. Cover the cat with three layers of strips. Leave to dry several hours.

8 Carefully cut out several strips of linen bandages from the piece of white fabric. Make each of the strips about 2 x 15cm in length.

9 Cover the head of the mummy cat with glue. Add strips of fabric across the cat's head as shown.

After a cat's body was wrapped in linen bandages, a face was drawn on its head. You could make your mummy cat look happy, like the one in the project. Alternatively, you could give it a more solemn expression like those seen on Egyptian statues of cats.

13 Place the cat on fabric. Cut a circle of fabric slightly larger than the base. Glue on a circle of white fabric to cover the base.

14 Paint features on to the face of your cat mummy. Use a fine paintbrush and black, brown and yellow acrylic paints.

27

Coffins and Cases

Dead bodies placed in shallow graves might accidentally be dug up by farmers ploughing their fields, eaten by wild animals, or stolen. In many civilizations, people believed that if a grave was disturbed and the bones were scattered, life after death would be impossible. This was why they took so much trouble to make special containers in which to store mummies and other human remains. There are several different words to describe these containers. Coffins, caskets and burial chests are all boxes with lids, usually made of wood. A sarcophagus is a covered chest made of baked clay or stone.

Coffins and other containers were designed in different shapes, according to the position of the body inside. The first Egyptian mummies were buried in a curled-up position, on their front or side. So their coffins were deep with rounded "roofs" and looked rather like little houses. Later, Egyptian mummy-makers arranged dead bodies stretched out full length. The coffins were shaped to look like people lying on their backs, waiting to be re-born in the next world.

▲ MUMMY'S EYE VIEW

If the eyes painted on the face of a mummy could really see, this would be the view from inside the dark, airless mummy case. The silent tomb in the heart of a pyramid would be decorated with magic spells, pictures of everyday life and dangerous adventures in the land of the dead. Statues of guardian gods often stood by to protect the spirit of the dead person.

▲ WRAPPED IN GOLD

The solid gold inner coffin of Tutankhamun is richly decorated with turquoise, lapis lazuli and other semi-precious stones. The coffin surrounded Tutankhamun's dried and shrivelled body and weighs a staggering 110kg. When archaeologists entered the young pharaoh's tomb in 1922, they found four gold-coated shrines, one inside the other. In the centre was a stone sarcophagus. Inside this were three more coffins, each shaped like a mummy. The one in the picture was the last they opened.

STRONG BOX ▶

A heavy stone sarcophagus housed the mummified body of the pharaoh Rameses II. The body was encased in several coffins inside. The word "sarcophagus" comes from two Greek words meaning "flesh-eater". This goes back to the time when the ancient Greeks lined their stone burial chests with powerful chemicals. These helped the flesh to dissolve away, leaving only clean, dry bones.

◄ MODELLED IN LIFELIKE PLASTER

Calm, yet solemn and watchful, this Egyptian woman gazes into eternity. Her head, neck and hands were moulded from stucco (painted plaster), then placed as a portrait on top of her bandaged, mummified body. This way of preserving people's likenessess after death was popular at the time the Romans ruled Egypt, from 30BC to the AD200s. The fine quality of the jewellery and craftwork used in her portrait indicate that she was a wealthy woman.

▲ A BOX OF GOLD

Containers for the dead could be big and splendid, or just big enough to contain a pile of ashes, such as this gold box. Small containers for ashes were needed where it was the custom to cremate (burn) a body before burial. This box contained the ashes of King Philip II of Macedon, father of the conqueror Alexander the Great, and was placed inside a marble sarcophagus. The starburst on its lid is the symbol of the Macedonian royal family.

HIDDEN ERRORS ►

An Egyptian mummy is wrapped in many layers of linen bandages, tied in place with strips of plant fibre. Ties and bandages held the body in place, but could also be used to hide any mistakes the mummy-makers might have made. Mummies that have been unwrapped have revealed skin stretched or burst by too much padding, broken limbs replaced by bits of wood, and heads fixed back on to bodies with sticks.

BURIAL URN ►

This urn (vase used for cremated ashes) was made by the Maya people of Central America around AD800. It is made from painted, fired pottery and decorated with the face of a goggle-eyed god. Usually the Maya buried their dead under the floors of their houses, or elsewhere in the ground. Occasionally, they placed them in caves which they believed to be gateways to the Underworld.

◄ BEAUTIFUL FOR EVER

A burial suit made of 2,160 pieces of jade tied together with gold wire was made for the Han princess Dou Wan. To the Chinese, jade was precious and magical with protective powers. Because it was so hard, they believed the suit would preserve Dou Wan's body forever, but in fact, the body rotted away. Dou Wan died in about 125BC.

A Model Worker

Figures called *shabtis*, like the model in this project, were buried in many Egyptian tombs. Their purpose was to serve as labourers in the afterlife. Egyptian people believed that they would be asked to work hard in the next world regardless of how rich or leisured they had been in their previous life. Osiris, the king of the Underworld, would call them to work, and had to be obeyed. So they had *shabtis* buried alongside them to do the work on their behalf. In the New Kingdom period, from 1550BC, some tombs had 365 *shabtis*, one for every day of the year, plus 36 overseers.

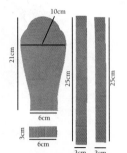

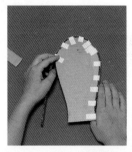

1 Fold corrugated cardboard in two pieces. Use a pencil and ruler to copy the shapes shown above on to the corrugated cardboard. Cut out the shapes.

2 Fix the 25cm strips of cardboard to the edge of each coffin base shape, as shown. Use small pieces of masking tape to hold the sides in place.

You will need: piece of corrugated cardboard at least 25cm x 16cm, pencil, ruler, scissors, masking tape, newspaper, 250g plain flour, 200ml water, fork, bowl, fine sandpaper, white, cream, blue, black and brown acrylic paints, thick, medium and fine paintbrushes, 240g self-hardening clay, modelling board, dish of water, dry brush.

5 Cover the top of the lid of the coffin with three layers of newspaper dipped in paste. Cover both the inside and the outside of the two halves of coffin.

6 Leave the coffin in a warm place to dry overnight. When completely hard and dry, sand the coffin and lid with the fine sandpaper.

7 Using white paint and a thick paintbrush, coat both halves of the coffin inside and out. Leave the coffin to dry for at least an hour.

Shabtis were made of wood, clay, wax, stone, bronze or faience (type of fire-glazed clay pottery). These shabtis are made of faience. Before around 1400BC, shabtis were shaped like mummies. Later, they were shown in ordinary Egyptian clothes. These shabtis, looking like royal mummies, were made for a priest and an admiral of the Egyptian navy.

11 Mould detail using water to wet the clay. Make a face and feet. Rub down with your fingers to smooth. Leave to harden and dry.

12 Paint the *shabti* cream and leave it to dry. To make the *shabti* realistic, use a dry brush to scuff the surface with blue paint.

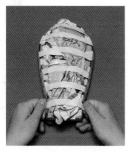

3 Tear and scrunch up strips of newspaper. Place them across the top of one of the coffin shapes to make the lid of the coffin and tape down.

4 Mix a thick batter-like paste with the plain flour and water. Use a bowl and fork. Tear up more strips of newspaper and dip each one in the paste.

Shabtis *were stacked in beautifully-decorated boxes usually made of painted wood to look like little houses. This shabti box is painted with a scene from the Egyptian Book of the Dead. The jackal-headed god Anubis weighs a dead man's heart to see is he is worthy of eternal life. The ibis-headed god Thoth records the judgement.*

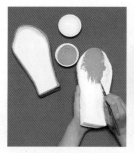

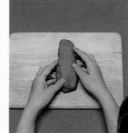

8 Leave the paint to dry. Use a thick paintbrush to paint the inside of the lid and base cream. Paint the outside of the coffin light blue. Leave to dry.

9 Draw a design on the coffin lid using a pencil. Use the fine paintbrush to paint your design with black paint. Follow the design in the final picture.

10 Now make a *shabti* from self-hardening clay. Shape the body using a little water, as shown.

The shabti you have made would have been buried alongside you, to do hard work on your behalf in the world of the dead. If you are feeling particularly lazy, you could make lots of shabti figures, for extra help!

13 Draw on features and clothes on the *shabti* with a fine pencil. Go over your design in brown and black paints using a fine brush.

14 Put the *shabti* in the finished coffin. Now it is ready to be buried as a hard-working model companion for a mummy.

Fit for a Pharaoh

The necropolis (city of the dead) at Giza in Egypt is one of the most famous burial places in the world. Three massive pyramids stand there, along with temples, boat-pits and many smaller tombs. There are also statues of guardian gods and a statue of the Sphinx (a lion with a human's head). Long causeways led to the pyramids. Mortuary temples, where bodies were prepared for burial, were built next to the pyramids.

Mummified bodies were ferried to Giza from royal cities and palaces on the opposite bank of the Nile. To the Egyptians, the East Bank of the river was the land of the living and of sunrise. The West Bank, where the pyramids stood, was the land of the dead and the land of the setting sun.

The largest pyramid at Giza, called the Great Pyramid, was built for Khufu, a pharaoh who ruled Egypt from about 2589 to 2566BC. Originally it was 147m high, nearly twice as high as the Statue of Liberty in New York, but some stones have been removed or have worn away. It was also covered in a gleaming outer layer of fine white limestone, but this, too, was removed. Over three million blocks of limestone were used to build the pyramid, each weighing about 2.5 tonnes. Inside there are two burial chambers, with a third unfinished burial chamber below ground level.

◄ DEAD END

Builders haul a giant block of granite along the Grand Gallery. Pharaoh Khufu has been laid to rest and they are sealing his burial chamber from the outside world. The gallery runs long and deep inside the pyramid. It leads upwards towards the burial chamber. Once the block has been put in place, the builders hope that anyone entering the Grand Gallery will think the passage is a dead end.

KEY
1. Outer layer of brilliant-white limestone
2. Mortuary temple
3. Causeway covered with white limestone
4. Tombs of Khufu's wives
5. Boat pits
6. Original burial chamber
7. Descending passage
8. Escape shaft
9. Queen's chamber
10. The Grand Gallery
11. King's burial chamber
12. Relieving chambers
13. Mysterious shafts
14. Granite block
15. Inner core of coarse limestone
16. Mastabas
17. Enclosure wall

◄ CITY OF THE DEAD

The Great Pyramid is the largest building in the necropolis. There are smaller pyramids for the pharaohs' queens and cemeteries packed with the tombs of royal family members and noblemen. Building stone and materials – as well mummified bodies – were carried from the riverside harbour along causeways to the pyramids. Builders were housed in on-site lodgings provided by the king. It took them at least 20 years to complete the work on the Great Pyramid.

◄ OFFERINGS

Priestesses perform the last funeral rites for Khufu in the mortuary temple. They will make offerings here every day following his burial, to help keep his spirit alive. The temple is on the eastern side of the Great Pyramid, because the Egyptians believed this was the direction of the rising sun and rebirth. It was built of fine white limestone with granite pillars and a gleaming floor of a black volcanic rock called basalt.

▲ WELL FURNISHED

Workers put the finishing touches to the pharaoh's burial chamber. The original contents of Khufu's chamber were stolen around 1000BC, but would probably have been similar to those found in the tomb of his mother, Queen Hetepheres. These still survive and include furniture of wood covered in gold, a bed draped with a canopy of luxurious linen cloth, and many other treasures.

Building a Pyramid

▲ STAIRS TO THE SHRINE
Workers carry heavy loads of mud brick and rubble up the steep steps to the top of a huge pyramid-shaped mound. They are barefoot to stop them slipping on the very steep steps. The place is the Mayan city of Tikal in Guatemala. The year is AD700. A queen has been buried inside the pyramid. Now the workers are building a shrine on top.

The Great Pyramid at Giza was built on foundations of solid rock. Before building could begin, however, the site had to be levelled (made absolutely flat). It would not have been possible to build the Pyramid accurately if the ground on which it stood had been uneven. All the corners had to be absolutely level with each other. Observations of the stars were then used to line up the four corners of the pyramid with north, south, east and west. The main building stone was locally quarried limestone. Interior chambers were lined with granite quarried at Aswan, 966km away, while fine white limestone covered the outer surface.

As the pyramid rose, the heavy blocks of stone had to be hauled up ramps. Without wheels or pulleys, everything had to be done by muscle power. The limestone blocks for the outer surface was polished smooth with small pieces of rock so that each piece fitted together perfectly with the next. A capstone stone) was dragged to the top. Finally, the ramps were demolished.

◄ FIRST PYRAMID DESIGNER
Imhotep was chancellor to the kings of Lower Egypt at the court of the pharaoh Zoser. He was also a scribe, doctor, priest and architect. Around 2650BC, he designed the huge Step pyramid at Saqqara as Zoser's tomb. It probably began as a *mastaba* – an older, rectangular type of tomb with sloping sides. Imhotep built six separate stone *mastabas*, piled one on top of the other. It became the world's first pyramid. When finished, it was 60m high.

▲ RECONSTRUCTING ANCIENT TECHNIQUES
The rough inner core of limestone blocks of a typical Egyptian pyramid has been exposed over the years. At the base, you can see some of the smooth slabs of facing stone that would once have covered it completely. The core stone is original and over 4,000 years old, but the facing stone is modern. It has been put there by archaeologists to help them study ancient Egyptian building techniques and to show visitors what the pyramids once looked like.

▲ A WILLING WORKFORCE

It could take 20 years to build a pyramid. Thousands of workmen toiled at the building site during the flood season of each year. At that time, their fields were covered with river water and they could not work on their farms. So they worked as labourers for the pharaoh as a way of paying their taxes. Other ways of paying tax included fighting in the army, or acting as messengers and labourers for government officials.

◀ LIGHT FOR WORK

Pottery lamps were used to provide light for workers in tombs deep underground. A wick of twine or grass burned in a pool of animal or fish oil. The light lasted as long as there was oil in the lamp, but was rather faint. Bundles of papyrus dipped in resin or pitch were also used as torches to light the way. These burned brightly, but the light was soon gone.

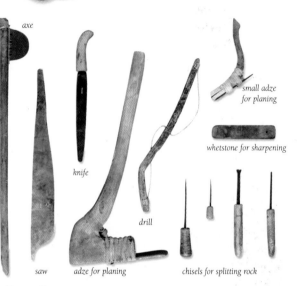

axe

knife

small adze for planing

whetstone for sharpening

drill

saw

adze for planing

chisels for splitting rock

▲ AT THE QUARRY

Giant blocks of granite in the quarry at Aswan, southern Egypt, bear marks made by workers over 3,000 years ago. The builders used balls of dolerite (a very hard rock) to pound the rock, and wooden mallets to drive wedges and chisels into the stone to split it. Large quantities of rough stone were usually quarried close to a building. Small amounts of good-quality stone, such as this granite, were carried along the Nile. They were used to line burial chambers inside the pyramids and for columns and statues in temples.

▲ BASIC BUILDING

The tools used by Egyptian workers were very simple compared with modern ones. Most were made of wood with blades of stone or soft metal, such as copper. No-one had discovered how to forge harder metals such as iron and steel, so tools had no sharp edges or long-lasting points. All the tools were powered by hand and muscle power. Egyptian workers had no big machines to help them.

THE LONG HAUL ▶

Many thousands of stone blocks were used to build a pyramid. Each might weigh over a tonne. The Egyptians had no cranes to help them move heavy weights into place. Instead, workers hauled blocks of stone up causeways of pounded earth using plant-fibre ropes and wooden rollers. As each pyramid grew bigger, the ramps grew longer and steeper. Hauling the top stones was very hard work.

A Lasting Memorial

Building tombs was a very costly business. They were often built when the person for whom they were intended was still alive. Many people spent huge amounts of money on beautiful tombs. For most of them, tombs were a way of telling others about what they and their family had achieved and of being remembered. Huge, permanent structures that were beautifully decorated gave out the message that an important person was buried there. They might serve as a memorial that could last for thousands of years.

Tombs were sometimes intended to be strongholds that kept the contents safe. Rich people hoped that a massive tomb, such as a pyramid or an earth mound, would protect their body and their treasures from grave robbers or anyone else who might seek to destroy them. Unfortunately, large monuments often acted like advertisements, attracting tomb robbers and trophy hunters eager to find valuable treasure hidden inside.

Many tombs were built close to temples. The temples were a link between the world of the living and the mysterious other world of spirits and gods. Offerings were made at the temple to the dead person's spirit and to powerful gods who might protect him or her.

▲ A Lasting Memorial

Queen Hatshepsut's mortuary temple is set into the cliff face at Deir al-Bahri. Hatshepsut was one of the few women to rule in Egypt, from 1473 to 1458BC. Like all pharaohs, she gave orders for work to begin on her tomb before she died. It was not a pyramid, but a room dug into a steep hillside. Her mortuary temple, which stands close by, is one of the most splendid in all Egypt.

◀ Palatial Tomb

The inner chamber of the rock-cut tomb of Rameses II is one of the best-preserved in Egypt. Rameses ruled Egypt from 1279 to 1213BC. His massive mortuary temple was laid out around two vast courtyards, entered through impressive gates. Next, there was a huge pillared hall, a shrine containing a sacred boat and a holy statue, and a sanctuary, where offerings were made.

▲ Homes for the Dead

The Etruscans, who lived in Italy from around 1100 to 100BC, dug large chamber-tombs out of tufa (soft, volcanic rock). In places where the rock was too hard to dig deep, they built tomb-houses up against natural cliff faces. The Etruscans designed the inside of their tombs to look like living people's houses. Tombs belonging to wealthy families were decorated with paintings and carvings, just like houses above the ground.

Signs of Life ▶

Wavy lines, diamond-shapes and triangles decorate stones at the entrance to a prehistoric tomb at Newgrange in Ireland. Like many other tombs built in Europe around the same time (about 3100BC), Newgrange was designed as a passage-grave. The burial chamber lay below an earth mound heaped 13m high. The entrance to the undergound chamber was through a narrow tunnel, to make it difficult for robbers to enter. A hole in the roof of the mound allowed the sun to shine into the burial chamber on 21 December, the sacred day of the winter solstice (the shortest day).

◀ Pacal's Monument

The Temple of the Inscriptions at Palenque, Mexico, was the tomb of the great Maya ruler Pacal, who ruled from around AD615 to 683. The tomb is named after the carvings and hieroglyphs (picture-writing) along the back wall of the temple at the top of the pyramid. The inscriptions record events in Pacal's life. The temple is built of limestone and looks white today, but originally it was painted red, the colour of blood and life. Pacal was buried in a huge limestone sarcophagus (coffin), also decorated with carved pictures and glyphs. A jade mask covered his face, and his body was sprinkled with cinnabar (a red mineral). The Maya believed this would guarantee his life after death.

◀ Ruler of All

Regiments of terracotta soldiers surround the burial place of Shi Huangdi, the first Chinese emperor, who died in 206BC. According to reports written at the time, the tomb was designed to look like a model of the empire that Shi Huangdi once ruled. It had rivers of mercury, mountains modelled in stone and constellations painted on the ceiling. The whole chamber was covered by a huge earth mound and set inside a large park surrounded by a high wall.

Tomb Decorations

Some of the world's most amazing works of art have been found in tombs. They have been hidden away underground, where no-one can admire them or wonder at the skill of the workers who made them. To many people today, this might seem an odd thing to do, but it made sense to people living in the past.

In ancient civilizations, a tomb was a home where a dead person would live for evermore. Naturally they wanted it to look as good as any house above ground. They employed the most skilful artists to cover the walls of their tombs with paintings and asked the best craftworkers to make clothes, jewellery and furniture. Often, wall paintings and objects put in the tombs were finely decorated with lifelike scenes. These may also have been designed to work sympathetic magic, that is, to try and make the good things of life happen in the afterlife by showing them in the paintings.

Tomb decorations and furnishings almost always carried messages. They reflected the religious beliefs of the person buried in the tomb and identified his or her rank or occupation and lifestyle. The tombs of rulers were often decorated with royal symbols, while warriors were usually buried with their swords.

▲ FINISHED AT LAST

After all the years of building work, everything is ready. Rich treasures to be placed alongside the pharaoh have been lovingly created, and the pharaoh himself has been mummified. Carefully, deep inside the pyramid, a worker puts the last stones in place, making sure that he closes off completely the Pharaoh's chamber from the outside world. Within, the Pharaoh waits to begin his journey through the Underworld.

▲ WELCOME TO THE AFTERLIFE

Ancestor figures line the walls of a tomb in the city of Monte Alban, Mexico. They are waiting to welcome a buried person to the world of the dead. These paintings were made by the Zapotec people, who lived at Monte Alban between AD100 and 900.

▲ ROYAL STANDARD

This panel shows rulers feasting and farmers presenting them with gifts of sheep and cattle. It was buried in a royal grave at Ur, the capital city of Sumer, a powerful kingdom which is now part of Iraq. Over 2,000 graves have been discovered there. Sixteen of them contain the remains of kings and queens, dating from 2600–2500BC, along with many wonderful treasures, such as a helmet made from the beautiful metal, electrum.

◀ DECORATED DOORWAY

A couple holding hands, and two graceful oryx (wild antelope) decorate a tomb entrance at Hili, in south-east Arabia. The hunters and farmers who lived there around 2500BC buried their dead in large communal tombs, made of carefully cut and shaped stone. Archaeologists have found many fragments of pottery and stone vessels inside the tombs. They have also found the remains of tall mud-brick towers used for storage, or possibly for defence.

▲ BREAKING THE CODE

The Egyptians used a form of picture writing known as hieroglyphs on important monuments and tombs. There were around 1,000 different hieroglyphic symbols. Each stood for an object, an idea or a sound. Only priests and specially trained scribes could read them. The Egyptians continued to use hieroglyphs for sacred inscriptions, but they developed two simpler ways of writing for everyday use. After the end of the Egyptian era, knowledge of how to read hieroglyphs was lost. Then, in 1789, a slab of rock, known as the Rosetta Stone. On it was an inscription in three languages, one of which was hieroglyphs, the second everyday Egyptian, and the third ancient Greek. Using the Greek letters as a key, French scholar Jean-François Champollion worked out what the hieroglyphs meant in 1822.

▲ LEISURE AND PLEASURE

Under a chequerboard ceiling, an Etruscan family and their friends enjoy a pleasant meal together. They are entertained by a musician playing a double flute. This burial chamber at Tarquinia, in Italy, is known as the Tomb of the Leopards. It was beautifully decorated with wall paintings around 400BC. The dead bodies buried there would have been arranged on couches, just like the diners shown in the painting.

FOR A NOMAD CHIEF ▶

Long-horned goats prance energetically across a saddle cover of woollen felt and leather. The cover was buried in the tomb of a nomad chief at Pazyryk in the Altai Mountains of Siberia, around 400BC. Textiles were among nomads' most prized possessions. They were light and easy to carry as the nomads moved around. Textiles usually rot away, but the cloth and leather items buried at Pazyryk were preserved because the tombs were frozen by the bitter Siberian winter soon after they were made.

Reflections of Life

The walls of many Egyptian tombs were covered with colourful pictures like the one in the picture below. These tomb paintings were more than decorations. They were designed to show how life should be continued after death. Each image of a person was meant to be a record of all that was best and most long-lasting about them.

The tomb paintings were very carefully made. First, the wall was coated several times with plaster. Then it was marked out in a grid-pattern to make sure that each part of the design fitted neatly into the available space. Junior artists sketched the picture in red paint. Senior artists made corrections and went over the outlines in black ink. Finally the outlines were filled in with paint. The panel on the page opposite shows how to draw figures in the Egyptian way. Egyptian artists drew each part of the body from its best angle.

You will need: *paper, pencil, black felt-tipped pen, ruler, red felt-tipped pen, large piece of thin white card, old bowl, 500g plaster of Paris, 200ml water, old wooden spoon, petroleum jelly, coarse sandpaper, cream, turquoise, red, blue, yellow, green, brown, gold and black acrylic paints, fine paintbrush, 25cm string, scissors, white fabric, PVA glue, glue brush.*

1 Draw a pencil design similar to that shown in the final picture. Go over it in black pen. Rule vertical lines 2cm apart and horizontal lines to make the grid.

2 Measure the maximum length and width of the design. Draw a box of this size on the card, then draw a wavy shape inside the box.

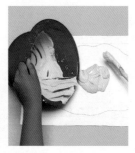

4 Smear a small amount of petroleum jelly over the card. Pour the plaster of Paris on to the jelly-covered area. This stops the plaster sticking.

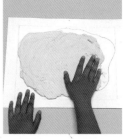

5 Spread the mixture to fill the wavy shape to a depth of about 8mm. Smooth the surface with your hand and leave to dry for two hours in a warm room.

This wall painting from the tomb of Nebamun, an Egyptian nobleman, shows him hunting in the marshes. He is accompanied by his wife, his daughter and the family cat. In his right hand he holds three herons as bait and in his left he holds a snake-shaped stick to throw at his quarry. Paintings like this tell us how the Egyptians hoped to spend their lives in the next world. They also served a magical purpose – birds and fishes were symbols of fertility, so they were also images of rebirth and new life.

9 Use a fine paintbrush to paint the background of the plaster cream. Paint around the design itself. Leave the paint to dry for at least an hour.

3 Mix plaster in a bowl, using a wooden spoon. The plaster should have a thick consistency and the mixture should drop from the spoon in dollops.

EGYPTIAN STYLE

1 To draw figures without a grid, use a pencil to draw the shapes shown below. Start with simple lines and circles.

2 Add features such as limbs and clothes, using the first lines as guides. Use an eraser to remove unwanted guidelines.

3 Add more simple lines. Draw a line across the robe and a tray on the shoulder. Round off the lines to make arms and legs.

4 Complete the design by drawing features on the face and food on the tray. It's easier to build up your picture this way.

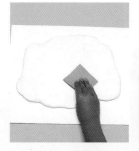

6 Gently rub the plaster with a piece of coarse sandpaper. Smooth the rough edges and all over the surface and sides of your slab of plaster.

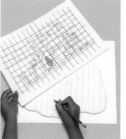

7 Use the ruler and pencil to draw a 2cm square grid on the plaster grid. Carefully remove your plaster from the piece of card by lifting one edge at a time.

8 Copy each square one by one from the paper design on to the plaster. Begin at the centre square and work outwards. Erase the grid lines.

10 Paint in detail using a fine brush. Paint the border using red, yellow, blue, green and gold acrylic paints. Leave the wall painting to dry.

11 Tie a knot in each end of the string. Cut two small pieces of fabric and glue them over the string to keep it in place and to hang your wall painting.

Egyptian tomb paintings were meant to be read like hieroglyphs. They often portrayed figures in stiff poses, like statues. But the paintings were carefully made. The artists hoped they would last for ever, and many have survived for thousands of years. They tell us a great deal about how ancient Egyptians lived.

Take it with You

Often, when someone died, the things that were important to them were collected together and buried with them. The tombs of kings and queens were filled with precious ornaments and jewellery, but also with everyday goods such as cups, jars, pots and knives intended to be used in the afterlife. Warriors and conquerors often had their weapons and armour buried with them.

The objects buried alongside a dead person are known as grave goods. They can tell us about past people's beliefs and ideas, about the development of technology, and the growth of trade. Even so, we have to be careful when looking at objects buried in the past. Many of them are luxury items, made only for the richest people. Ordinary people might have used the same kind of things, but made of cheaper materials and with simpler decorations.

▲ TRANSPORT ALONG THE NILE

A worker on the way to the pyramids looks down at a village on the banks of the river Nile. Most ancient Egyptians lived in clusters of small, mud-brick houses, close to the river, which provided water for their crops and homes. The river was the main means of transport, too. Sailing boats carried traders, fishermen and government officials on business. Most Egyptians enjoyed their way of life so much that they hoped it would continue after death, for ever.

▲ FOR A GOOD NIGHT'S SLEEP

Lions keep watch while a kneeling figure supports a curved headrest. This very ornamental object comes from the tomb of the Egyptian pharaoh, Tutankhamun. Ordinary Egyptians slept with their heads supported on similar stands, although theirs were not as highly decorated as this one, and were made of cheaper materials. Headrests look awkward, but they could be surprisingly comfortable to use. They kept the neck and shoulders cooler than thick pillows on hot summer nights and also protected elaborate hairstyles.

SEATED IN STYLE ▶

This graceful wooden armchair looks almost too beautiful to sit on. It was made to furnish the tomb of Princess Sitamun, aunt of pharaoh Tutankhamun, around 1365BC. It is carved from precious imported ebony, inlaid with ivory, and decorated with gold. Its feet are shaped to look like lion's paws. Elegant furniture like this was only made for royal palaces and tombs. Ordinary Egyptian families had simple chairs, stools and beds made of plain wood or woven reeds.

◄ READY TO WRITE

This case containing reed pens and an inkwell was found in the tomb of an Egyptian scribe buried around 30BC. Even after death he would have been as prepared for making notes or recording royal commands as he had been in life. Scribes were the best-educated people in Egyptian society. Many were royal officials and one, called Horemheb, even became pharaoh. Scribes wrote on papyrus (paper made from pressed reeds) using ink made from soot.

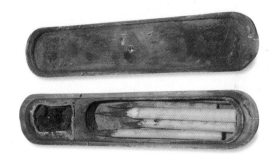

TREASURES FROM FAR AWAY ►

We do not know exactly how this Etruscan bronze jug and basin, or this Greek pottery vase, ended up in a Celtic princess's tomb in France. They must have been taken to France by traders and were probably bought and sold several times along the way. They would have been traded for such goods as furs, honey, grain and amber. The bronzework was made in Italy and the pottery was made in Athens. All three objects would have been very rare in Celtic Europe and highly prized by people living at the time (around 500BC). That is why they were placed in a position of honour inside the royal tomb.

DEADLY DAGGER ►

A gilded iron dagger was buried alongside a Celtic chieftain at Hochdorf in Germany, around 500BC. It tells us about Celtic metal technology and also about Celtic beliefs. Its blade has been broken and twisted. This may have been to kill its power, so that it could rest in the grave and do no further harm. The Celts believed that the time soon after someone's death was dangerous for their relatives and friends. For a while, the dead person's spirit remained trapped close to the body, and might hurt passers-by.

CHINA'S BEST CHINA ►

Porcelain (delicate pottery) fruits were made for the tomb of Zhu Yeulian, an emperor of the Ming dynasty. His family ruled China from 1364 to 1644. After the emperor died he expected to live in the grand style he was used to, forever. His tomb contained 500 porcelain models of courtiers as well as a porcelain copy of his carriage. Models were put in royal tombs to represent real objects. The porcelain showed off the emperor's wealth and, unlike the real objects, was everlasting.

Food for Thought

We all need food to stay alive. Many ancient peoples thought it would be needed in the next world, as well. They often buried stores of real or model food, and sometimes drink, alongside dead bodies in graves. The ancient Egyptians made cakes in the shapes of spirals, doughnut-like rings, and pyramids. They would have used honey as a sweetener, as sugar was unknown to them. Priests and priestesses regularly left food at important tombs long after a dead person's funeral ceremony. These offerings were a way of honouring a dead person's spirit and of helping it to stay alive.

Many ancient cultures painted pictures of feasts and made little models of farm workers, cooks and servants for their tombs. They hoped these would work in a magical way to help nourish the dead.

You will need: pencil, ruler, A5 white card, scissors, 110g butter, 110g caster sugar, mixing bowl, wooden spoon, fork, egg, small bowl, 270g plain flour, board, rolling pin, pastry cutter, non-stick baking tray, currants, oven glove, cooling rack.

1 Use a pencil and ruler to draw a grid of 2cm squares on white card. Copy the shape of the crocodile in this picture on to your grid, one square at a time.

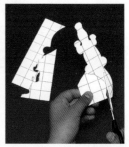

2 Use scissors to carefully cut out the shape of the crocodile. Cut slowly around the corners so that the shape is as smooth as possible.

4 Use a fork to beat an egg in another bowl. Slowly add the egg to your butter and sugar mixture. Stir the mixture with the wooden spoon.

5 Add the flour and fold it in. This releases bubbles and thickens the mixture. To make crunchy cookies cut and fold the mixture slowly.

Model bakers are hard at work, grinding flour, kneading dough and shaping it into loaves. Painted wooden models of houses, farms and everyday occupations were placed in the tombs of people who could not afford top-quality wall paintings. They were meant to recreate life in the world of the dead. While they were alive, the Egyptians ate a lot of bread, made from emmer (an early kind of wheat) or barley. Bread was nourishing, but could be hard to eat – it contained grit from grinding stones and sand from the desert. Loaves of bread over 3,000 years old have been found in some Egyptian tombs.

9 Lay the crocodiles on a non-stick baking tray. Mark a scaly decoration with a cocktail stick on their bodies. Pre-heat an oven to 190°C/250°F/Gas 5.

3 Mix the butter or margarine and the caster sugar into a mixing bowl. Cream the mixture together with a wooden spoon.

MORE TASTY TREATS

1 To make other shaped cookies, draw a grid of 2cm squares. Copy the shapes shown below to your grid and cut out.

2 Make the pastry as shown in the main project. Place your cut-out cat on the dough. Cut out three or four cat shapes.

3 Place the fish template on to the dough and cut out three fish. As before, add currants to the shapes for eyes.

4 Bake in the oven (190°C/250°F/Gas 5) for 20 minutes. Remove from oven and leave to cool before eating.

6 Divide the cookie dough into two pieces. Then divide it into as many pieces as you want cookies. If you want eight crocs, divide it into eight pieces.

7 Sprinkle some flour on a board. Use a rolling pin to roll out the dough to a thickness of about 8mm. Press it down evenly to make the mixture smooth.

8 Place the crocodile shape on top of the dough. Use a pastry cutter to cut round the outline. Be sure to cut right through the dough to the board.

10 Give the crocodiles eyes by placing currants on their heads. Place the cookies in a pre-heated oven (190°C/250°F/Gas 5) and bake for 20 minutes.

11 When the cookies are done, ask an adult to remove the baking tray from the oven. Leave on a cooling rack for 20 minutes. They're ready to eat!

The ancient Egyptians feared that crocodiles would eat them. Several mummies have been found with evidence of injuries caused by crocodile bites. With these biscuits, you can enjoy eating crocodiles, instead!

Buried Treasures

In some ancient societies, people thought that it was more important to take their wealth with them on their journey into the next world than to leave it behind for the living to enjoy. Precious goods, especially if they were gold, acted as a badge of rank. They were meant to ensure that the dead person would be treated with as much respect in the afterlife as they had been on Earth. In many civilizations, precious stones were also believed to have protective powers and were buried in tombs to guard and help the dead.

Rich and powerful people sometimes took more than gold and jewels with them. Trusted bodyguards and personal servants were some of the most valuable possessions that a king or queen could have. Many rulers measured their wealth by counting the number of soldiers or slaves they could command. Servants were killed and buried alongside their master in order to serve them in the next life. One Sumerian queen was buried with her ladies of the court, all beautifully dressed, with ribbons in their hair. Pottery cups from which they probably drank deadly poison lie scattered around the floor of the tomb.

▲ SKILLED IN STONE

A Chinese craftworker carefully sews together small squares of jade with gold wire to construct a burial suit for his lord. He uses a circular knife to cut and shape the jade and a bow-drill to bore holes for the gold thread. Jade is a very hard stone and difficult to work. Skilled workers trained in handling precious jade were employed in factories attached to royal palaces.

▲ SEAT OF POWER

Four gold and lapis lazuli cobras rear up their heads on the back of pharaoh Tutankhamun's throne. Like many other animals that decorated the tomb, they had protective powers. Cobras were feared for their poisonous bite. Tutankhamun's tomb contained a throne because he was ruling pharaoh when he died. It was shaped like an armchair and covered with valuable coloured glass, semi-precious stones and silver, all set in gold.

◄ FIT FOR A QUEEN

This magnificent headdress was found on the body of a high-ranking court lady at Ur. She was buried in the grave of a Sumerian queen who died around 2500BC. The bodies of other courtiers and royal servants were found in the tomb, along with soldiers of the guard. In the grave there were also two carts drawn by six bullocks, plus their drivers and grooms.

▲ GLITTERING GOLD

Pectorals (chest ornaments), such as this finely-made golden disk, were proudly worn by Zapotec people. After death, they were a sign of honour and respect for a dead body. This pectoral was found at Monte Alban, Mexico, the Zapotec capital from 200BC to AD700. Zapotec people also made offerings to gods and ancestor spirits by throwing treasures into cenotes (water holes).

▲ FROM EVERYDAY LIFE

Warriors fighting animatedly decorate this gold comb from a Scythian chieftain's tomb. The Scythians were warlike nomads who lived on the shores of the Black Sea from around 700 to 300BC. They were famous for their horse-riding skills. They buried important people in deep, wood-lined tombs. Many Scythian gold treasures are decorated with scenes that the artists would have seen in everyday life. They showed wild creatures, valuable horses, people making clothes or milking animals, and soldiers fighting.

▲ RICHEST AND BEST

This massive collar of gold, coloured glass and semi-precious stones was made in the shape of the vulture-headed Egyptian goddess Nekhbet. It is another treasure from pharaoh Tutankhamun's tomb, one of the richest collections of ancient Egyptian art ever found. Tutankhamun lived when Egyptian craftworkers were at the peak of their skills. His tomb contained almost 2,000 objects including statues, thrones, musical instruments, weapons, jewellery and magic amulets, as well as his mummified body.

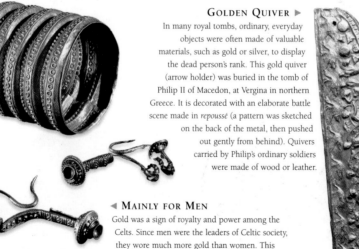

GOLDEN QUIVER ▶

In many royal tombs, ordinary, everyday objects were often made of valuable materials, such as gold or silver, to display the dead person's rank. This gold quiver (arrow holder) was buried in the tomb of Philip II of Macedon, at Vergina in northern Greece. It is decorated with an elaborate battle scene made in *repoussé* (a pattern was sketched on the back of the metal, then pushed out gently from behind). Quivers carried by Philip's ordinary soldiers were made of wood or leather.

◀ MAINLY FOR MEN

Gold was a sign of royalty and power among the Celts. Since men were the leaders of Celtic society, they wore much more gold than women. This gold bracelet and these two golden clasps were found on the body of a Celtic chieftain buried at Hochdorf in Germany around 500BC. They are valuable pieces of jewellery that he would have worn when he was alive. Workshops close by the tomb produced many extra ornaments of decorated sheet gold made for him after his death. They were fitted to his dagger, his weapons, and even his shoes, before burial.

Ornamental Touches

The Egyptians loved jewellery when they were alive and a great deal of jewellery has been found in tombs. Some is beautifully made from precious stones and costly metals. Other pieces are much simpler, and are made from materials such as pottery and bone. The falcon necklace in this project is based on a Egyptian design made using a technique called *cloisonné* (a framework of gold divided into separate parts that were filled with coloured glass or semi-precious stones). Gold was mined in large quantities in Egypt, but some gems were imported. Blue lapis lazuli had to be brought from what is now Afghanistan.

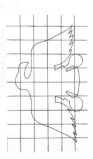

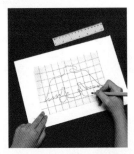

1 Draw vertical lines 2cm apart and then horizontal lines 2cm apart to make the grid, as shown. Copy the design above on to the grid, a square at a time.

2 Place the tracing paper over the design. Use masking tape to secure it. Use your pencil and ruler to trace the design and the grid on to the tracing paper.

You will need: *pencil, ruler, A4 paper, A4 tracing paper, scissors, rolling pin, one packet of self-hardening clay, modelling board, masking tape, modelling tool, cocktail stick, medium paintbrush, blue, red, green and gold acrylic paints (or gold paper if you prefer), white spirit, clear wood varnish, pen, PVC glue, 90cm string.*

This affectionate scene from a panel on Tutankhamun's throne shows Queen Ankhesenamun, the pharaoh's wife, gently spreading holy oil on her husband's chest. The panel is decorated with orange-red carnelian, green feldspar, light blue turquoise and rich blue lapis lazuli. It also gives us a picture of fashion around 1350BC. The pharaoh is wearing a pleated kilt and his queen is dressed in a flowing dress of white linen. They are both wearing gold sandals, short wigs, jewelled headdresses and collars and bracelets of gold and semi-precious stones.

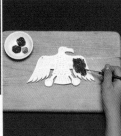

7 Leave the clay eagle to dry in a warm room. Use a medium paintbrush and blue acrylic paint to colour the eagle. Leave it to dry.

8 Use red, blue, green and gold acrylic paints, to decorate the eagle, as shown above. Make your eagle look as if it is made of gems and gold.

12 When the glue is dry, remove the tape and paint the paper tubes with red, blue and gold dots, as shown. You now have 50 beads to make a necklace.

13 Cut two lengths of string, each 45cm long. Thread one end of each string through the holes in the eagle's wings. Tie a knot in the strings.

3 Use scissors to carefully cut out the eagle shape from the piece of tracing paper. This forms the template from which to cut out your shape from the clay.

4 Place the self-hardening clay on a board. Use a rolling pin to flatten it out. Roll the clay to about 5cm deep and 21cm x 15cm in size.

5 Tape the tracing paper to the clay. Then use a modelling tool to carefully cut around the outline of the eagle. Make sure you cut right through the clay.

6 Remove the tracing paper. Use the modelling tool to mould detail. Use a cocktail stick to make a 3mm hole on each wing, 2cm from the top edge.

9 Clean the paintbrush in water. When the painted eagle is dry, dip the clean brush in wood varnish. Gently glaze the model all over.

10 Paint five 5cm square pieces of paper blue and five gold (or use gold paper). Cut each into strips 1cm wide. You need 25 strips of each colour.

11 When the strips are dry, roll around a pen. Dab glue to the ends of the paper to stick. Use masking tape to secure the paper until the glue dries.

Rich jewels, fashioned into designs like your necklace, were worn as signs of wealth and rank, or to display good taste and a love of beauty. Simpler jewels were given by ordinary people as tokens of love, or worn as examples of the maker's own craft skills.

14 Thread the beads on to the strings. Alternate the colours. You should have 25 beads on each string to make a decorative necklace.

15 Finish threading all the beads. Tie together the ends of the two pieces of string in a secure knot. Trim off any unwanted string to neaten.

Honouring the Dead

A s far as we know, almost all past civilizations have held some sort of funeral ceremony to say farewell to their dead. Sometimes these have been simple occasions, but at other times they have been much more elaborate, with many different people and processes involved. The way funerals are organized, prayers were said and rituals performed depend on each civilization's own religious beliefs. Most funerals, however, share the same purpose. They showed that the dead person was separated from the living world. The funeral eased the person's passage from this world to the next, and helped them find new life.

Studying funeral customs can help historians find out more about past societies. In a civilization where everyone was equal, funerals were mostly the same for everyone. However, in a society such as that of ancient Egypt, where there was a huge gap between rich and poor, the grandest funeral ceremonies were reserved for the rich and powerful.

In some societies, dead people continued to play an important role even after they were buried. Many civilizations, in South America and Asia for example, honoured the spirits of ancestors and asked them for protection and advice. Some West African cultures believed that dead ancestors were reborn as babies, ready to play a new part in family life.

▲ TO A TOWER TOMB

Slowly the body of an Inca noble wrapped in cloth is carried through village streets to a *chulpa*, its final resting place. *Chulpas* were tall stone towers used to bury important people in ancient Peru. The dead person's face was covered by a clay mask or precious metal and valuables were arranged next to the body. When an emperor died, some of his wives and servants were killed to keep him company in the next world.

▲ OPENING THE MOUTH

Egyptian mourners take part in the final ceremony, called Opening the Mouth, before a mummified body is laid to rest. The mummy's coffin was held upright by a priest wearing the mask of Anubis, the god of the dead. The ears, eyes and mouth were touched with magic implements. Purified water was scattered and incense burned. Egyptians believed this ceremony helped the mummy hear, see and speak in the next world.

▲ JOURNEY TO THE TOMB

This is part of a wall painting that shows some of the people who took part in an Egyptian pharaoh's funeral procession. The coffin, carried on a sledge, was placed in a boat. It was surrounded by attendants and by women mourners, weeping and wailing. Royal servants carried food, drink and treasures to place in the pharaoh's tomb. Priests said prayers and burned incense. They poured milk in front of the sledge as an offering to the gods.

▲ FEASTING WITH THE DEAD

Dressed in their best, Aymara people from Bolivia visit the graves of their ancestors on the Day of the Dead. They carry with them bread and other gifts to leave as offerings to the dead people's spirits and to honour their memory. Today, this custom is combined with the Christian festival of All Souls' Day. It is, however, a continuation of a custom that has existed for thousands of years in many Central and South American countries.

▲ A CONSTANT REMINDER

Funeral effigies (models of dead people) stand guard outside tombs cut deep into the rock at Tanatoraja on the island of Sulawesi, Indonesia. Effigies served as a constant reminder of the dead person to friends and family who were still living. Sometimes they also provided a home where a dead person's spirit could live. A fine effigy was often a source of family pride. It linked living descendants to famous dead ancestors and allowed them to share in their ancestors' glory.

◀ A FINAL RESTING PLACE

A warrior and his son from the Dani people of Irian Jaya, Indonesia, honour the remains of their dead ancestor. Long ago, the dead man's body was smoke-dried to preserve it, then laid to rest in a cave. Wells, water holes, crevices in the rocks and caves were all favourite places for bodies to be left after funeral ceremonies were completed. Many people believed that they were entrances into the next world.

▼ DEATH RIDER

These model skeletons on horseback decorate a tomb for the Mexican Day of the Dead. Mexican people believe that dead spirits return to life on that day, and share in celebrations with their living friends and relatives. As well as decorating tombs, Mexicans also leave gifts of sweets, bread and drink at gravesides, for the dead spirits to enjoy. They add bunches of strong-smelling marigolds. Their scent is believed to attract spirits from the world of the dead.

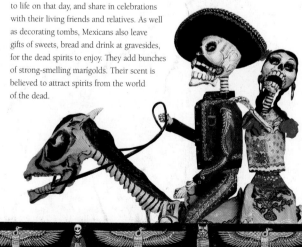

Best Clothes

Preparations for many funerals involved washing or embalming the dead body, then wrapping it in a shroud (sheet of clean cloth) or dressing it in special clothes. This project shows you how to make a beautifully decorated cloak similar in style to those worn by the Incas of South America. Dressing the body in special clothes showed respect for the dead person. It was also a way of preparing them for the next world. In many cultures, people mourning a dead friend or relative also wore special clothes. In addition, women mourners might cut their hair, scratch their cheeks or smear their faces with ashes.

1 Use scissors to carefully cut the red felt material to size. Use fabric cutting scissors if you have them or sharp, paper scissors, but get an adult to help.

2 Use the ruler to measure a length of white fabric. Use the fabric scissors to carefully cut out the material. This will be used as a decorative border.

You will need: tape measure, piece of red felt 116cm x 113cm, scissors, ruler, piece of white fabric 116cm x 20cm, long piece of white felt 116cm x 10cm, pencil, scrap paper, black, yellow, red, blue and gold acrylic paints, medium and fine paintbrushes, PVA glue, glue brush, corrugated cardboard, wooden kebab stick.

7 Leave the black paint to dry. Then using the fine paintbrush, paint in alternate blocks of yellow colour. Leave the fabric to dry.

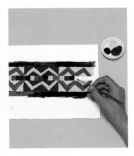

8 Carefully fill in the rest of your design using red, yellow and black acrylic paints as shown. Leave the fabric to dry in between each colour.

This modern reconstruction is designed to recreate the spectacle you would have seen if you had visited Cuzco (the Inca capital city) on a religious festival day around AD1500. Then, the mummified bodies of Inca rulers, dressed in fine robes, were carried shoulder-high through the streets in a grand procession. In many ways, the Inca peoples treated dead rulers as if they were still alive. As well as giving them new clothes from time to time, they offered them food and drink and even asked their advice on important topics.

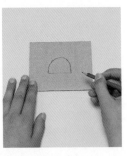

12 To make a fastening, use a pencil to draw a semi-circle shape on to a piece of corrugated cardboard. Make the shape about 4cm across.

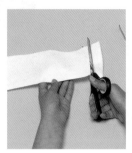

3 Now use the tape measure to measure a piece of white felt about 116 x 10cm. Use the scissors to carefully cut out the shape from the felt.

4 Use a pencil and ruler to draw a 1cm border at the top and bottom of the white fabric (not the felt). Work on a flat surface.

5 Using a pencil and ruler, draw the design of triangles and squares. Follow the pattern shown above by marking along a central line, every 5cm.

6 Place a piece of protective paper on a surface. Colour the border with black acrylic paint and a medium paintbrush. Try not to go over the rest of the design.

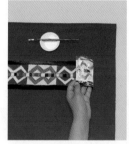

9 When the paint is totally dry, peel it back and brush glue on the back. Glue the border lengthways along the short edge of the red felt, 30cm from the edge.

10 Brush glue over the back of the strip of white felt. Stick down on to the red felt, about 20cm in from the painted border.

11 Lay the blanket decorated side up. Fold the edge over so that the fold runs through the length of the white felt, as shown above.

13 Put a blob of glue in the middle section of the cardboard. Push a wooden kebab stick about 15cm long in to the glue and leave it to dry.

14 Paint the pin using bright colours such as blue, red and gold. Leave to dry before attaching to your cloak. Close the cloak and fasten.

To wear your ceremonial cloak, fasten it as the Incas would have done with the large wooden or metal pin. Among the Inca, rulers, rich nobles and people sacrificed to the gods were dressed in beautiful woven cloaks. Inca patterns were usually based on geometric patterns, such as zig-zags or squares, or on stylized birds, animals and people.

Spells and Curses

▲ LUCKY CHARM

To the Egyptians, scarab beetles were sacred. They symbolized the sun god. Scarab beetles made little balls of dried dung, which they rolled along the ground. The Egyptians believed the sun god rolled the sun across the sky in the same way every day. Model scarabs, like this glazed pottery one, were worn as amulets (lucky charms) to protect the wearer from harm. Embalmers wrapped scarab amulets in a mummy's bandages to guard the dead person in the next world.

People from many different civilizations have often been terrified of meeting spirits of the dead that have returned to the living world. They have feared that ghosts or spirits who are not resting peacefully in their graves, or enjoying life in the next world, will come back to haunt the living and do harm by bringing diseases and disasters with them from the world of the dead. To guard against these dangers, people prayed and performed rituals. They carried lucky charms, such as stones, bones, little figures or magic symbols, to protect themselves from harm. Many funerals have also included ceremonies to make peace with the dead person's spirit.

This fear of ghosts and spirits was often put to a practical use. It kept tomb-robbers away and frightened people who wanted to use parts of a dead body to make sinister medicines, or perform magic spells. Tomb-robbing was considered a serious crime in Egypt, where it was believed that the gods would punish such criminals in the next world. Despite fears of the dead, however, for centuries tombs have been robbed in every culture around the world.

A FALSE RUMOUR ▶

The Earl of Caernarvon was a keen archaeologist. He was also a very rich man and helped pay for the expedition, led by Howard Carter, that discovered Tutankhamun's tomb in 1922. He died soon after helping Carter investigate Tutankhamun's amazing treasures. Some people said that his death was caused by the Mummy's Curse. In fact, Caernarvon died from a serious infection caused by a mosquito bite. However, many people take the idea of Tutankhamun's curse seriously, even today.

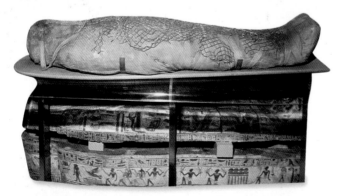

◀ BEAUTIFUL BEADS

This mummy, displayed on a modern stand above its painted coffin, was given magical protection by beautiful bright blue beads. They were made of faience, a type of fine, glass-like pottery, made from crushed quartz mixed with lime and plant-ash, and covered with a shiny glaze. Faience was widely used for jewellery in ancient Egypt, as it was much cheaper than precious stones. It was also used for beads and amulets designed to protect mummified bodies, and living people as well. Often, these amulets were shaped like gods of the dead, such as Anubis, or like hieroglyphs standing for important ideas, such as *Ankh*, which means life.

◀ MISTAKEN IDENTITY

Little cloth figures like this one were buried in many tombs from the Chancay civilization, which flourished in Peru from around AD1000 to 1450. At one time, people thought they were either toy dolls, or else little mascots, buried to bring good luck to dead people. In fact, we now know they were model servants, placed alongside the corpse to serve the dead person in the next world.

▲ FAITHFUL SERVANTS

Sinister secrets are often linked to burial sites. It was said that the designer and chief builders of Emperor Qin Shi Huangdi's tomb in China were buried alive inside it, along with the emperor's body. That way they could not reveal its secrets to any living soul. We do not know whether this story is true, because archaeologists have not yet excavated the emperor's burial chamber. However, they have found the remains of horses that had been buried alive on the outer edges of the tomb.

▲ SPINE-CHILLING STORIES

Mummies have fascinated writers and film-makers for many years. Most books and films about mummies have been horror stories. They describe terrible disasters that befall explorers who break into mummies' tombs, or dreadful things that happen when a monstrous, evil mummy mysteriously rises from its coffin and comes to life. A few films about mummies, however, have been light-hearted, like this one by the comedy duo Abbott and Costello, made in the 1950s. It was designed to make people laugh at silly and superstitious mummy tales.

▲ GRAVE GUARDIAN

An Egyptian snake goddess called Meretseger was said to protect the Valley of the Kings. Many pharaohs were buried in the valley, along with their valuable grave goods. The Egyptians believed that Meretseger, whose name means 'she who loves silence', lived on the mountain shown here, which rises above the Valley of the Kings. Meretseger was extremely dangerous and her presence on the mountain made the Valley a place to be avoided by those who wanted to be spared Merteseger's anger.

Re-entering Tombs

There have been tomb-robbers for almost as long as tombs have been created. Monuments full of riches, such as pyramids, were clearly visible to treasure seekers. Even when tombs were hidden underground, their location was usually known to local people. Many tombs were entered and robbed, often soon after they were completed. By 1000BC, the pyramids at Giza and most of the tombs in the Valley of the Kings had been robbed of their precious contents.

From the 1700s onwards, wealthy European collectors visited places rich in remains, such as Egypt and Italy, and paid for private excavations. Sometimes, they dug carefully, recording all the details of the site. Often, however, they just paid local workmen to dig for buried treasure. Many of the objects they found went on public display in stately homes or museums. They inspired great interest in the past and admiration for past cultures, but often valuable information about the site was destroyed. Since the 1920s, however, archaeology has become more scientific. Archaeologists take care to record exactly what they find. Today, when a tomb is discovered, the site is protected to prevent thieves from stealing the contents.

▲ ROBBING THE DEAD

As the light from his torch flickers across the richly decorated walls, an ancient Egyptian tomb-robber peers into the burial chamber he has just entered. Many Egyptian tombs were robbed, often soon after they were completed. The robbers, driven by poverty or greed, risked the anger of the gods and fearful punishments.

▲ AN EXCITING DISCOVERY

A group of archaeologists at work on the excavation of Sipàn, a important tomb site in Peru. In 1987, the tombs were originally found by grave-robbers, who fell out with each other before one informed the police. The site was sealed off and a 24-hour armed guard was posted to prevent more looters destroying the site further.

MEASURING THE VIEW ▶

French army engineers and architects began a survey of Egyptian ancient buildings in 1798. From the early 1700s, European travellers to Egypt had brought back enthusiastic reports of all the treasures they had seen. After the French, led by General Napoleon Bonaparte, invaded the country, the amount of information about Egypt in Europe greatly increased. Egyptian styles and designs became the latest fashion in art, interior design, jewellery and clothes.

◀ UNTOUCHED FOR CENTURIES

This photograph, taken in 1922, shows workers uncovering the entrance passage to Tutankhamun's tomb. Howard Carter, who led the excavations, discovered the tomb on 4 November 1922. A set of rock-cut steps led to a plastered doorway covered in official seals. The doorway had been placed there by ancient Egyptian priests and guards about 3,500 years ago. It led to a corridor at the end of which was another sealed door. Carter made a tiny hole in this and when asked what he saw, replied, "wonderful things".

▲ PACKING UP

The treasures discovered in Tutankhamun's tomb had to be carefully wrapped and packed in cases before they could be transported to the museum in Cairo. It took two years to clear all the objects in the tomb before the lid of Tutankhamun's outer coffin could be raised. Inside was a beautifully decorated second coffin, inside which was a solid gold coffin. When the lid of this final coffin was raised, it revealed the body of the king with a magnificent mask covering his head and shoulders.

THE LORD OF SIPÀN ▶

The royal tombs at Sipàn on the coast of Peru were made by the Moche people around AD100 to 600. Excavations are still continuing, but already two magnificent tombs have been found there. One contains the body of a ruler, buried in a wooden coffin filled with treasure. Archaeologists have called him the Lord of Sipàn. Around his coffin were five other bodies (one with a dog), who were probably servants. A guard with his feet cut off, perhaps to stop him running away, lies at the entrance to the tomb.

◀ STOLEN TREASURE

The face of a snarling jaguar decorates a gold bead from the Moche royal tombs at Sipàn. To the Moche, jaguars were powerful spirits closely linked to their chiefs and rulers. The grave-robbers who broke into the undisturbed tombs hastily stole all the gold and silver objects they could find. They were sold to rich collectors in Peru and elsewhere. This prevented archaeologists from accurately reconstructing the contents of the tombs.

Unravelling the Past

In the 1900s, archaeology became more scientific than ever before. Excavators now use many techniques to survey a site and explore the soil before they start digging. Aerial photography is used in an aircraft high overhead to take images of the ground that can reveal traces of buildings, roads and fields. Electric currents can tell surveyors what lies beneath the surface. Archaeologists can also work out scientifically how old an object is. Dendrochronology uses the growth rates of tree rings to date wooden objects. Radio-carbon dating measures the amount of carbon (C-14) in an organic object (wood, bone, hair). It can do this because all living things contain C-14, which decays at a known rate after a living thing dies. Archaeologists use scientific information, together with traditional types of evidence, such as pottery, to piece together the puzzle of the past.

Ancient objects must be preserved to stop them decaying further. They may be cleaned, disinfected, freeze-dried, injected with chemicals, preserved in liquid or stored in controlled environments where temperature and humidity (moisture in the air) can be constantly monitored.

▲ FACE TO FACE

The mummy of the pharaoh Rameses II was so well made that we can still look at his proud, rather austere face today. We can imagine what he must have looked like when he was alive over 3,000 years ago. Archaeologists who removed the bandages from Rameses' mummy found that the eye-sockets had been packed with wadding to preserve the shape of his face and to stop the natron (salt) mummifying solution from destroying his features once the eyeball had been taken away. An X-ray revealed a small bone had also been inserted to maintain the shape of his nose.

▲ BEFORE...

This is the skull of a young woman named the Ice Maiden by archaeologists. She lived in about 400BC in the Pazyryk region of Siberia on the border with China and Mongolia. Soon after she was buried, water seeped into her tomb. It froze, preserving her body and the textiles and leather objects she was buried with until their discovery in 1993. The find provided archaeologists with information about the people of this remote region.

▲ ...AND AFTER

This clay model shows how Russian expert Dr Kozeltsiv thinks the Ice Maiden looked while she was alive. Using a plaster cast of her skull and careful measurements of her teeth and bone structure, he has reconstructed her face by adding layers of muscles modelled in clay and a fine covering to look like skin. He has also added eyes made of glass and a braided wig of long, dark hair.

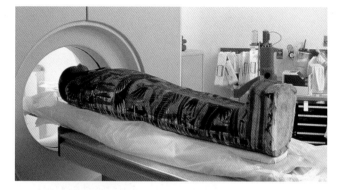

◄ INSIDE STORY

Sophisticated machines such as this CAT (Computer-Aided Tomography) scanner can help archaeologists see inside a mummy. The CAT scanner was first invented for medical investigations, but it is very useful to archaeologists. They can use the scanner to look inside a mummy or other dead body without damaging it by unwrapping it or cutting it up. CAT scanners make maps of tissues inside the body and build up lifelike pictures of organs, muscles and bones. Other medical techniques, such as X-rays and ultrasound, can also help archaeologists investigate bodies from long ago.

◄ VIRTUAL MUMMY

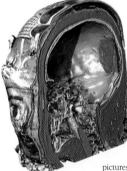

This image of an Egyptian mummy was created as part of the Virtual Mummy Project at Frankfurt University, Germany. The project aims to use computer mapping and modelling to draw three-dimensional pictures of the inside and out-side of a mummy. The images are based on photographs, X-rays and detailed measurements.

◄ A DIFFERENT VIEW

Once the virtual reality images of the mummy have been created, they can be moved round and even opened-up on screen. This means that all interested students can obtain detailed, realistic information about the mummy without damaging it. This is a great improvement on earlier ways of examining and studying mummies. More traditional techniques of investigation have disturbed and sometimes even destroyed old and delicate objects.

◄ THE SOURCE OF KNOWLEDGE

Glass cases filled with exhibits from ancient Egypt line the corridors of the Belvedere Palace in Vienna, Austria in 1875. Visiting museums was a popular pastime among educated middle-class people throughout Europe, and displays about ancient Egypt were especially popular. Many private and public collections paid large amounts of money to purchase Greek, Roman and Egyptian objects from professional treasure hunters working overseas. Ever since they were created, these collections have given archaeologists valuable opportunities to learn more about the past and helped them to understand the significance of new discoveries as they were made.

Timeline

Humans have been burying their dead in many different ways for more than 100,000 years. In certain times and places they have chosen to preserve the bodies of their dead by mummifying them. However people have decided to remember those who die, the remains that have survived tell us much about past ways of life.

100,000–28,000BC

c. 100,000BC THE FIRST-KNOWN BURIALS, by prehistoric people in Qafzeh (present-day Israel).

c. 70,000–40,000BC NEANDERTHALS living in several different parts of Europe bury their dead in caves, sometimes in family groups. At Shanidar the presence of pollen suggests that flowers were put in the graves with the dead.

c. 28,000BC AN ADULT MAN and two children buried with lances of mammoth-ivory, thousands of ivory beads that once decorated their clothes, jewellery, and an ivory figurine found at Sunghir (near Moscow).

Siberian baby mammoth

28,000–10,000BC

c. 10,500–8500BC THE NATUFIAN PEOPLE OF THE LEVANT (present-day Israel, Jordan and Syria) dress their dead in jewellery made from shells and bones.

c. 10,000BC CEMETERIES ARE DUG IN NUBIA containing burials of war-dead. Today, archaeologists find arrowheads still embedded in skeletons' bones.

2500–1700BC

c. 2500BC NOMADS ON THE STEPPES (wide grassland plains) of Russia and Central Asia bury their dead in deep pit graves.

c. 2133–1786BC TOMBS OF LOCAL GOVERNORS and others high in the social hierarchy at Beni Hasan, Egypt, are decorated with wonderful wall-paintings showing scenes of warfare and everyday life.

c. 2060–1786BC SECOND, less important, age of pyramid building in Egypt (Middle Kingdom).

Egyptian ibis container

1700–1390BC

c. 1600–1027BC RULERS FROM THE SHANG DYNASTY in China are buried in tombs containing rich grave-goods and oracle-bones (examples of early Chinese writing). The rulers' wives and servants are killed and buried alongside.

c. 1570BC FROM NOW ON, the mummified bodies of important Egyptians are buried in tombs cut into mountain-sides, or in pits.

c. 1390–332BC (NEW KINGDOM) Egyptian priests bury mummified bodies of bulls sacred to the god Apis in the Serapeum – a specially cut series of underground passages close to the royal burial ground at Saqqara, near Memphis, Egypt. In the Late Period, they also buried mummified cows, baboons, hawks and ibises in underground galleries.

Egyptian mask

1390–1000BC

c 1362BC PHARAOH AKHENATEN and his courtiers are buried in rock-cut tombs on the outskirts of Aketaten, the new city he founded. Their tombs are decorated with carvings in a revolutionary new artistic style.

c. 1350BC WARRIOR-KINGS AT MYCENAE in Greece are buried in tall, beehive-shaped tombs called *tholoi*.

c. 1327BC THE MUMMIFIED BODY of Pharaoh Tutankhamun is buried along with magnificent treasures in a tomb deep in the Valley of the Kings, on the West Bank at Thebes, Egypt.

500–450BC

c. 500–400BC THE GRAVES OF IMPORTANT PEOPLE in Ancient Greece begin to be marked with a tall, carved stone, called a stele. Often, this bears their portrait, or an inscription praising them.

c. 480BC A CELTIC PRINCESS is buried at Vix, eastern France. Her tomb contains jewellery, including a necklace of pure gold weighing over half a kilo.

c. 450–250BC HIGH-RANKING PEOPLE from the Moche culture are buried at Sipan, northern Peru. Their bodies are wrapped in fine cloth, and surrounded by precious jewellery and pottery.

Celtic bracelet

450–400BC

c. 450–50BC CELTIC WARRIORS in northern and central Europe cut off the heads of their enemies and preserve them in oil. The warriors believe this gives them power.

c. 400–300BC NOMADS living near Pazyryk, in the Altai Mountains of Siberia, bury their dead chiefs in shaft-tombs dug into the ground. The tombs are then covered with earth mounds, and topped by rocks. Because of the severe Siberian weather, they freeze, keeping the bodies inside well preserved until today.

helmet from Ur

c. 400BC–313AD ROMANS bury their dead alongside main roads leading out of Rome.

400–300BC

c 395–332BC MUMMIES MADE IN EGYPT are buried in cases decorated with beautiful, lifelike portraits of the dead people.

c 350BC A MAGNIFICENT TOMB is built for Mausoleus, King of Caria at Halicarnassus (near Bodrum, Turkey). It is 50m high and topped by a pyramid. It becomes one of the Seven Wonders of the World. After this, the word mausoleum is used to describe any splendid tomb built above ground.

336BC KINGS OF MACEDONIA are buried with their weapons and armour, as a sign of their military strength while alive.

late Egyptian mumm

AD250–600

c. AD250–500 JAPANESE RULERS are buried in tombs topped by vast mounds of earth, up to 2,500m in circumference and 20m high. They contain clay *haniwa* (guardian) figures of soldiers, shamans, entertainers and court ladies.

c. AD250–900 MAYAN RULERS of Central America are buried in pyramid-shaped tombs, which also serve as temples for ancestor-worship. Some of the largest and most splendid are at Copan (Honduras) and Tikal (Guatemala).

Swedish helmet

AD600–690

AD618–906 WEALTHY PEOPLE ruled by the T'ang Dynasty, in China, are buried in tombs alongside lifelike models of people and animals, modelled from clay and glazed in glowing colours.

c. AD620 ANGLO-SAXON KING RAEDWALD is buried inside his ship, surrounded by weapons and jewels, at Sutton Hoo on the coast of East Anglia. The acid soil destroys his body, but the metal and stone treasures survive.

AD690–800

AD692 MAYAN PRINCE PACAL is buried in a stone sarcophagus, wearing a jade mask. His tomb is hidden deep under the floor of a pyramid-shaped temple at Palenque, Mexico.

Chinese model chariot

c. AD800 A WEALTHY OFFICIAL OR NOBLEMAN from the Igbo-Ukwu people, in Nigeria, West Africa, is buried seated in a wooden chamber. One of his feet is resting on an elephant tusk, and he carries a staff in his right hand. He is wearing thousands of beads.

10,000–3500BC

c. 6000–5000BC PEOPLE IN JERICHO (present-day Jordan), bury the skulls of dead ancestors beneath the floors of their homes.

c. 6000–1500BC CHINCHORRO PEOPLE (of Chile) make elaborate mummies, and dress them with wood or clay face-masks, and wigs.

c. 4000–1000BC PEOPLES IN PREHISTORIC EUROPE build chamber tombs of boulders or slabs of rock. Some are covered by huge mounds of earth, now known as barrows or tumuli.

European barrow tomb

3500–2600BC

c. 3500BC WORLD'S LONGEST-PRESERVED MUMMY made at Chinchorro, Chile.

c. 3500–2181BC MASTABA (BENCH) TOMBS built in Egypt. They are low, rectangular, and have flat tops and stepped or sloping sides. The most elaborate are made for bodies of pharaohs of the First Dynasty (c. 3100–2682BC.) Early *mastabas* were made of sun-baked mud brick; by 2,600BC, some were made of stone.

c. 2630BC ACCORDING TO TRADITION, the Egyptian architect Imhotep designs the first step pyramid as a tomb for the body of Pharaoh Zoser at Saqqara, near Memphis, Egypt.

2600–2500BC

c. 2600–2181BC PEAK AGE of pyramid-building in Egypt.

Egyptian gold collar

c. 2566BC THE GREAT PYRAMID is completed as the tomb to house the body of Pharaoh Khufu. At 147m high and with a base 230m square, it is still the largest stone pyramid in the world and the only one of the Seven Wonders of the Ancient World still surviving.

c. 2500BC KINGS AND QUEENS of the city of Ur (in present-day Iraq) were buried with fabulous golden treasures. Their servants committed suicide, and were buried with them to serve them in the next world.

1000–900BC

1000BC–AD100 THE ADENA PEOPLE of the Ohio Valley, North America, make huge earth mounds, up to 20m high, to cover tombs built of logs.

c. 900BC SARCOPHAGUS (stone burial chest) of King Ahiram, found at Byblos (present-day Lebanon), is decorated with one of the earliest known inscriptions using the Phoenician alphabet, on which the letters of the modern Western (Roman) alphabet is still based.

c. 900–200BC THE PARACAS PEOPLE in Peru bury their dead wrapped in beautiful cloth, patterned with tiny pictures of magic animals.

Paracas mummy

900–700BC

c. 800–50BC IN THE CELTIC CULTURE in northern and central Europe, important people are buried on wagons, surrounded by weapons and treasures, in wood-lined graves covered by tall earth mounds.

c. 700BC A VERY RICH KING OF PHRYGIA (ancient state of Asia Minor) is buried under a 53m-high earth mound near what is now Ankara, Turkey. Legends told that he was the famous King Midas, who was so rich because everything he touched turned to gold. More probably, the Phrygian king was one of Midas' ancestors.

700–100BC

c. 700–100BC THE ETRUSCANS (early inhabitants of central Italy) cut tombs out of rocky hillsides to look like underground houses. Rich families have tombs with several "rooms", all beautifully decorated with paintings and carvings. Inside, there are lifelike statues of the dead.

c. 700–300BC SCYTHIANS (nomads who lived near the Black Sea) bury their dead chiefs in deep pits, with the chiefs' wives, servants, and sumptuous gold jewellery. The chiefs' horses and grooms were sacrificed and buried nearby.

Etruscan bronze

300–200BC

c. 300BC–AD50 PEOPLE OF THE DONG-SON CULTURE in south-west China make delicate bronze statues to bury in tombs, showing scenes of daily life, battles and religious ceremonies.

c. 300BC–AD200 RULERS AND RICH MERCHANTS living in the desert city of Petra (present-day Jordan) are buried in beautifully decorated tombs cut deep into the rose-red rock of their city.

206BC HUANGDI, FIRST CHINESE EMPEROR, is buried in a magnificent tomb guarded by 6,000 lifesize terracotta soldiers, near Xi'an, central China.

Chinese jade suit

200–12BC

202BC–AD220 WEALTHY PEOPLE IN CHINA, ruled by the Han dynasty, build richly furnished tombs, decorated with wall-paintings, sculpture and lifelike clay models of houses and farms.

c 200BC–AD800 THE ZAPOTEC RULERS of Monte Alban (in Oaxaca, present-day Mexico) build carved and painted tombs. Jewellery and valuable pottery is buried with them.

12BC ROMAN TRIBUNE (government leader) Gaius Cestius is buried under a huge pyramid-shaped monument. (Egyptian styles are popular after Rome conquers Italy in 30BC.)

AD1–250

c. AD1–750 THE NAZCA PEOPLE of southern Peru bury their dead in stone-lined cysts (chambers) dug into the ground. The bodies are arranged in a sitting position and wrapped in cloth; sometimes pottery is buried alongside.

Celtic burial chamber

c. AD100 THE PEOPLE OF SAN AUGUSTIN, Colombia, South America bury huge stone statues (half men, half monsters) alongside their dead.

c. AD100–400 CHRISTIANS IN ROME bury their dead in narrow underground passages, called catacombs.

AD117 ROMAN EMPEROR HADRIAN is buried in a huge, marble-covered tomb in Rome.

AD800–900

c. AD800–900 A MAYAN KING (possibly Yax Pac, called Rising Sun) is buried in a pyramid tomb decorated with more than 2,500 glyphs (picture symbols) in the city of Copan (in present-day Honduras).

c. AD800–1100 THE VIKING PEOPLES of Scandinavia bury their most important chiefs and royalty in ships, placed in the ground, or in stone enclosures.

AD809 CALIPH HARUN AL-RASHID dies. He is ruler and spiritual guardian of the mighty Muslim empire, based in Baghdad (Iraq). His tomb in the city of Mashad, Iraq, soon becomes a place of pilgrimage.

Chinese grave guardian

AD900–1400

AD940 MUSLIM RULERS from the Samanid dynasty in Central Asia build brick-walled tombs in Bukhara, Uzbekistan.

c. 1000–1500 CHRISTIAN KINGS AND QUEENS are buried in churches, usually with a life-size effigy (statue) of themselves on top.

1368–1644 RULERS FROM THE MING DYNASTY in China build a series of splendid tombs at Nanjing. They are guarded by huge magic beasts.

c. 1400 THE INUIT PEOPLE of Greenland preserve dead bodies by placing them in clefts in cliff-faces.

Chancay (Peruvian) grave servant

AD1400–1900

c 1438–1532 THE INCA PEOPLE of Peru preserve the mummified bodies of dead rulers and honour them. They parade the dead rulers through their capital city, Cuzco, on religious festival days.

Taj Mahal mausoleum

1631–1648 AD MUGHAL emperor SHAH JAHAN builds the Taj Mahal (near Agra, India) as a tomb for his beloved wife. Many people say it is one of the most beautiful buildings in the world.

1600–1900 MUMMIES wearing their everyday clothes are still made in Sicily, southern Italy.

GLOSSARY

afterlife
According to many ancient beliefs, another world where people continued to live after death.

amulet
A lucky charm, often in the form of jewellery worn around the neck or wrist.

ancestors
Dead members of your close family.

boat pit
Place close to an Egyptian temple where a funeral bark was buried.

bow drill
A tool used for making holes in wood or stone that looked rather like a bow used to shoot arrows, and was powered by pulling the bowstring.

burial chest
Box with a lid where a body was placed for burial.

CAT scanner
A machine which uses an electronic system called Computer-Aided Tomography (CAT) to create a series of pictures showing the inside of a living or dead body without the need to cut it open.

capstone
The topmost stone placed on a pyramid to finish it.

cartouche
An oval line that Egyptian scribes drew round an inscription to show the person being named is important.

casket
A container for a dead body, usually made of wood, with a lid.

cauldron
A large cooking pot.

causeway
A raised roadway.

Celtic
From the civilisation of the Celts, a people who lived in Europe from around 800BC– AD100.

cenote
A natural water-hole.

chamber
Another name for a room.

chulpa
A stone tower where important Inca people were buried.

cloisonné
A metalworking technique in which objects are covered in a brightly-coloured enamel (jewel-like glass) separated by strips of polished metal.

cobra
A poisonous snake found in Africa and Asia with a flat area that grows behind its head.

coffin
A box with a lid, used to contain a dead body for burial in a grave.

cremated
Burned at great heat until only ash remains.

dissect
To cut up in order to study, usually for medical purposes.

crook
A long stick with a wide hook at one end used by shepherds to catch (and sometimes rescue) sheep.

cryogenic
At a very low temperature, cold enough to freeze a body so that it is preserved.

dendrochronology
The science of dating wooden objects using tree-ring patterns made as trees grow.

dolerite
An extremely hard, smooth rock. Lumps of dolerite were used by the Egyptians as hammers.

ebony
A valuable, dark, shiny wood from a tropical tree.

effigies
Models of dead people.

embalming
Soaking or injecting a dead body with chemicals to preserve it.

faience
Brightly-coloured pottery with a shiny finish, also used to make jewellery.

flail
Two short sticks, joined together so that one of them can move easily, used to strike harvested wheat repeatedly in order to separate the wheat grains from their stalks, used as a symbol by the pharaohs.

funeral
A boat made from tree bark, or a model boat, used to carry the bodies of dead Egyptians to their tombs.

funeral rites
Prayers, ceremonies and offerings to the gods when a dead body was buried.

gilded
Covered with gold.

glyphs
Picture writing.

granite
A very hard, shiny stone that can be carved and polished to reflect the light.

grave goods
Items, often of great value, buried alongside a dead body in a grave.

hieroglyphs
A complicated system of picture-writing used by Egyptian scribes.

inscription
Letters or picture-writing, often carved on stone tombs or monuments.

ivory
The hard, white material from which elephant and walrus tusks are made.

jackal
A wild animal related to dogs that lives by hunting and by scavenging (searching for scraps of dead bodies to eat.)

lapis-lazuli
A deep blue semi-precious stone.

limestone
A fairly soft, usually white or honey-coloured stone, that is easy to carve.

monument
A building or statue designed to help living people remember a dead person and what they did.

mortuary temple
A temple built close to a tomb where offerings were made by priests to a dead person's spirit.

natron
A natural chemical, rather like salt, found in the Egyptian desert.

necropolis
A collection of tombs all in one place.

nomad
A person who does not have one particular settled home, but who travels regularly between several different places.

ochre
Red earth, often used to make paint.

organs
Parts of the body that keep it alive, such as the heart, lungs, brain or stomach.

papyrus
A substance similar to paper made from strips of reeds (river plants) soaked with water then pressed together.

passage grave
A grave entered through a narrow tunnel.

pectoral
Jewellery worn on the chest.

plaster cast
A model made by pouring a mixture of plaster (finely-powdered chalk and limestone) and water into a hollow space, and letting it harden. When dry, the plaster stays in the shape of the space it was poured into.

quiver
A container for arrows.

resin
Gum produced by plants and trees that sometimes has germ-killing powers.

sarcophagus
A strong stone box with a lid, used to contain dead bodies.

scarab
A dung-beetle honoured as a symbol of the sun-god by the Egyptians. Model scarabs were carried as lucky charms.

shabti
A model figure, placed in Egyptian tombs, to work on behalf of the dead person during the afterlife.

shrine
A holy place where offerings were made, often to an image of a god or goddess.

sphinx
A monster with a human head and a lion's body, a symbol of royal power to the Egyptians.

sympathetic magic
Ceremonies designed to make something happen by doing a similar action. For example, priests sprinkled a few drops of water on the ground to encourage the rain to fall.

terracotta
Baked clay, usually reddish-brown in colour, used for pots and sculpture.

turquoise
A semi-precious, pale blue-green stone.

underworld
The place where people believed the spirits of dead people went after they died. There were many different beliefs about the underworld. To some peoples, the underworld was a spirit's final destination. To others, it was a place where a spirit passed through on its way to a new life after death.

urn
A pot or vase used to contain the remains of a dead person.

INDEX